Global Business

Theme 4 for Edexcel Business A Level Year 2

Alan Hewison

Nancy Wall

Alan Hewison is an experienced teacher and has been a senior examiner of economics and business for many years. He has been involved with the development of some of the new economics and business courses and has written several other revision guides and textbooks.

Nancy Wall was a teacher for 15 years. Since 1991 she has worked in curriculum development, with a particular interest in teaching strategies and classroom resource development. She is currently reviews editor of 'Teaching Business and Economics', the magazine of the Economics, Business and Enterprise Association. She has long experience of writing and editing resources for students.

Acknowledgements

We are grateful to Paul Rapley for reading and commenting on many chapters.

Every effort has been made to trace the owners of copyright material, but in a very few cases this was not possible. We offer our apologies to any copyright owner whose rights may have been unwittingly infringed.

© Anforme Ltd 2016
ISBN 978-1-78014-034-6
Images supplied by Shutterstock.com

Anforme Ltd, Stocksfield Hall, Stocksfield, Northumberland NE43 7TN.

Typeset by George Wishart & Associates, Whitley Bay.
Printed by Potts Print (UK) Ltd.

Contents

Using this book

This book covers Theme 4 of the Edexcel's A Level Business course. Much of the new content is best understood if you can link it to the ideas that figured in your earlier work in the subject. To help you revise, we have put reminders at the head of many chapters. They list the topics that are treated as prior knowledge required. Sometimes you will find page numbers cross-referencing earlier work in this book, so that you can remind yourself about relevant content. Other page numbers will take you to a helpful definition.

As you approach the end of the course, you will find that you need to draw on information from different topics in order to write really good answers. Sometimes useful terms appear in the margins – they will remind you of the ideas that you need to draw on to write really good assessments and evaluations.

This book is likely to go out of date rather quickly. There is a lot happening just now. The impact of Brexit on the business world is very difficult to forecast and businesses are going to have to cope with very significant uncertainties. We do not yet know how the exit is going to be accomplished. Probably, little will happen until decisions are revealed. So you still need to know how the EU works.

Similarly, the global economy is changing, creating more unknowns. (See page 107, Current Trends, for a summary of the way economic growth rates and trade appear to be slowing as of late 2016.)

So what should you do? Be very sure to keep up with events and changes as they occur – follow the news. Each time another change occurs, ask yourself, what businesses will this affect, and how? Look for solid evidence whenever possible, to help illuminate controversial issues. Remember too, that Europe has not yet fully recovered from the impact of the Financial Crisis of 2008-9. The UK and many other countries are still unwinding its consequences.

Secondly, revise steadily all the time. The things you can remember from past work will help you to understand much of what you are learning now.

Exam style questions
These are to be found at the end of some chapters (but not all). Some have a mark scheme that is very like those of Paper 1 and Paper 3. (None of them have been written by your examiners so they are rough guides rather than specimen questions.)

Other questions are rather different from Edexcel's questions but have a mark scheme to give you an idea of the length and depth that your answer should provide. A few questions are designed to help the learning process rather than to help with exam technique. Some of the questions cover topics from previous work.

Lastly, don't just read this book! Get information from other sources. It isn't hard to find. Enjoy the course and good luck to you all.

Chapter 1

Growing economies

Mature economies

Low incomes

Rising productivity

Growth rate of the UK economy compared to emerging economies

A good look at the business cycle shows that GDP does not grow at a steady rate. There are fluctuations in the rate and the economy can even shrink if growth is negative.

Official figures show that the UK economy grew by 2.2% in 2015, after rising by 2.9% in 2014. Growth in the economy is measured by changes in Gross Domestic Product (GDP). This shows the total value in monetary terms of all the goods and services produced in an economy over a period of time, usually a year or a quarter (three months).

Discussion point

Why do you think economic growth is considered important by the government?

What is the likely impact of economic growth on individuals and businesses?

We can group economies according to their level of development. Some became industrialised in the 19th century (developed economies), some over the past 50 years (emerging economies) and some still have very small industrial sectors (developing economies). Within each category, businesses vary considerably as to the environments in which they operate. It helps to describe them in terms of the relative significance of their primary, secondary and tertiary sectors.

The primary sector involves the production of raw materials and includes agriculture, mining and quarrying and fisheries. The secondary sector involves manufacturing and the production of tangible goods. The tertiary sector involves services and knowledge-based industries.

Developed economies are often described as mature. They have a relatively high standard of living with generous welfare provision. Only a tiny proportion of the working population will work in the primary sector, although output may be significant due to labour saving machinery and extensive use of fertilisers. Around 70% or more of the working population will be producing services. The rest – perhaps 10-25% of the workforce – will be employed in manufacturing. The developed economies include Europe, North America, Australia and Japan. Production will often be capital intensive because wages are high and capital equipment is relatively cheap. Most people will have some skills and many will be highly educated.

● **Developing economies** still have very large primary sectors and relatively small secondary sectors. Incomes are mostly very low; for some, economic growth is slow. Most economic activities will be labour intensive because capital equipment is expensive and probably imported. Many Asian, African and Latin American economies are still developing. Where there are wars, starting a business may be difficult or impossible.

● **Emerging economies** have some features of both developed and developing economies. Their economies are growing fast, sometimes with rapidly rising standards of living. There will be growth in the secondary and tertiary sectors; expansion will usually be fastest in manufacturing. People will migrate from the countryside to urban areas. As investment in capital equipment grows, production becomes less labour intensive and productivity will rise, although the equipment may be less sophisticated than that of developed countries. Trade will be expanding rapidly. This group includes China, India, Nigeria, Indonesia and Vietnam amongst others.

Developed economies have high per capita incomes, literacy levels and life expectancy. Typically, they have large service sectors. Other important indicators relate to health care and welfare provision.

Developing economies generally have low incomes, weak education and welfare systems, abundant cheap labour and relatively little capital investment. Setting up new businesses may be both risky and difficult. Where there is manufacturing, it may be mainly of clothing and footwear.

Emerging economies have rising levels of capital investment and growing, increasingly productive secondary sectors. International trade is growing rapidly and leading to economic growth. They diversify into new lines of production, often in collaboration with multinational corporations (MNCs). They are attractive as both production locations and growing markets.

Table 1: UK and selected emerging economies, GDP annual growth %

	Average 2006-15	2006	2007	2008	2009	2010	2011	2012	2013	2014	2015
Brazil	2.1	4.0	6.1	5.2	-0.3	7.5	2.7	0.9	3.0	0.1	-3.9
Nigeria	5.0	2.7	6.3	5.4	4.3	4.9	7.8	7.0	6.3	6.8	8.2
India	6.5	9.3	9.7	5.3	7.4	10.1	7.3	5.1	5.6	7.2	7.6
China	7.7	12.7	14.3	9.6	9.2	10.4	9.3	7.7	7.7	7.3	7.6
Vietnam	5.0	7.0	7.1	5.7	5.4	6.4	6.2	5.2	5.4	6.0	6.7
UK	0.7	2.8	3.4	-0.8	-5.2	1.7	1.1	0.1	2.2	2.9	2.2

Source: The World Bank

Economic growth rates

Table 1 shows that the UK, the mature economy, grew much more slowly than the emerging economies. This was despite the UK having had some very good years. There is nothing odd about this. Mature economies in reasonably good times when the global economy is fairly stable tend to average 2-2.5% economic growth per year. Emerging economies can grow much faster over a period when they are 'catching up'.

Singapore and South Korea are now classed as developed because of their very rapid growth in the last 40 years. The transition from a developing to a mature economy involves big increases in productivity as workers migrate from farming communities to urban manufacturing and service sectors. Typically, the process takes 30 years or more.

Show your understanding

1. To what extent were the emerging economies affected by the financial crisis of 2008-9?

2. Compare their experience to that of the UK.

Commodity prices

China and India were responsible for much economic growth after 2000; growth is slowing a little in China but both still have comparatively strong growth rates. Nigeria has experienced rapid growth; the increase in GDP in 2004 was an astonishing 33.7%! It is now the largest African economy, having overtaken South Africa in 2014, but by 2016 it was suffering very seriously from falling oil prices. Vietnam is expanding rapidly as more and more businesses take advantage of its cheap labour supply. In some sectors such as footwear and clothing it is taking business away from China. Brazil's experience was different again; it has a less open economy than other emerging economies and depends very heavily on exports of primary products, both agricultural and mineral. If commodity prices are rising the Brazilian economy will grow but if not, then the growth rates will fluctuate. This is what happened in 2015; commodity prices fell and the situation was made worse by a political crisis.

Growing economic power: the BRICs

In 2002, it was clear that a number of countries were developing fast. The most striking were Brazil, Russia, India and China – partly for their sheer size and partly for their speed of growth. Jim O'Neill, a distinguished economist then working for the investment bank Goldman Sachs, named them the BRICs. (The group sometimes includes South Africa, which is the most developed African country.)

BRICs

The distinguishing feature of the BRICs is that they collectively transformed global trade relationships. From 2000-10, they were responsible for between one third and one half of global economic growth. Trading relationships between the developed economies and the rest of the world changed dramatically. However, economic growth rates slowed after 2011. This may be because the catch-up process was coming to an end for China and Russia. Political issues might explain fluctuations in India and Brazil.

The CIVETs

The acronym CIVETs was coined by Robert Ward, of the Economist Intelligence Unit, in 2009. The CIVETs are six emerging economies – Colombia, Indonesia, Vietnam, Egypt, Turkey and South Africa. They are said to be the next wave of rising economies after the BRICs. These countries are grouped together for several reasons. They have fairly sophisticated financial systems, controlled inflation and rapidly increasing, and predominantly young, populations. They are not reliant on any one sector. They also have problems in common, such as corruption and income inequality. (Economy rankings below are all based on current GDP figures.)

Columbia – the 41st largest economy in the world with a population of over 48 million. It is the third largest exporter of oil to the US and also produces gold and coal.

Indonesia – the 16th largest economy in the world with a population of over 260 million. The country is the largest economy in Southeast Asia and a member of the G20 major economies and the Association of Southeast Asian Nations trade bloc (ASEAN, see page 30).

Emerging economies

Vietnam – the 47th largest economy in the world with a population of over 92 million. It is also a member of ASEAN and has made huge progress since the extreme poverty of the 1980s. Its strength is in manufacturing and cheap labour.

Egypt – the 31st largest economy in the world with a population of over 90 million. It relies heavily on tourism (currently under pressure from terrorism) and has a good port network and potentially huge gas reserves.

Turkey – the 18th largest economy in the world with a population of over 80 million. A member of the G20, it might apply to join the EU, with which it has strong trade links. This could take a long time.

South Africa – the 40th largest economy in the world with a population of over 48 million. The most developed country in Africa, it has large mineral reserves of all kinds, including gold and diamonds.

MINTs

Not be outdone, Jim O'Neill then came up with another acronym, MINT, which stands for Mexico, Indonesia, Nigeria and Turkey. In many ways these countries have similar characteristics to the CIVETS, and of course they share two of the same countries.

Mexico – the 15th largest economy in the world with a population of over 125 million. It is part of the North American Free Trade Association (NAFTA) which attracts many foreign companies to set up production there.

Nigeria – the 21st largest economy in the world with a population of over 185 million. Its manufacturing sector is the third-largest on the continent, and produces a large proportion of goods and services for the West African region.

Find out

Research the CIVETs and MINT countries:

1. What are the economic growth rates for the most recent year available?

2. How are their rankings expected to change by 2050?

3. What are the implications of their growth for British businesses?

Implications of economic growth for individuals and businesses

Economic growth means that the economy is producing more than it did before. To do this it needs to use more resources, which will include labour. Jobs are created and incomes rise, which in turn can lead to increased demand and further growth.

In emerging economies this process can have startling results. Economic growth in China and now countries like Vietnam has created employment opportunities where none existed before. According to the International Labour Organisation (ILO), China's urban population has grown by 440 million since 1979. Many Chinese left a life of subsistence farming to move to the cities, taking employment in the ever increasing number of factories springing up as China entered a period of rapid economic growth.

Rising incomes

As economies like China develop, workers with increased disposable income begin to spend and consume more goods and services, often ones that they have never experienced before. The demand for fridges, cars, clothes and all sorts of consumer goods that have high income elasticity of demand begins to rise. This provides growth opportunities for businesses, both domestic and foreign.

The Pentland Group

The Pentland Group is a conglomerate company that started in 1932 as a shoe wholesaler in Liverpool. Amongst other brands it owns Speedo swimwear and Berghaus outdoor clothing. In 2014 it recorded a 36% rise in profits, thanks largely to an increase in demand from Chinese swimmers. Sales of its products have been strong in China and it has also seen increasing success in other emerging markets such as Brazil, Russia and Turkey.

In 1964 it became one of the first European companies to use global sourcing by getting shoes manufactured in Asia. Fuelled by this access to cheaper labour, the company has grown rapidly over the years through a series of takeovers and licence deals. It owns a range of sports and fashion brands, including Mitre footballs, Canterbury rugby kit, Red or Dead, Ellesse and Kickers.

1. Explain possible reasons why the Pentland Group has seen "increasing success in emerging markets."
2. How has global sourcing helped the Pentland Group?
3. What impact might this global sourcing have on the Asian countries that make the shoes?

Cutting costs

Individuals benefit from job opportunities and rising standards of living. Economic growth raises incomes, but in time, it also raises wage costs. Businesses that outsource their manufacturing processes have moved around in order to find the lowest labour costs. Consumers gain while cost-conscious businesses keep a watchful eye open for new cost-cutting opportunities.

Examples

As of 2014, Nike products were manufactured in 150 footwear factories in 14 countries. To start with, over half of production took place in China, now only 25% comes from there. 43% of production takes place in Vietnam, where wages are lower.

Apple's biggest supplier of manufactures is Foxconn, which is Taiwan-owned and operates mainly from China's Pearl River Delta region. While Apple has been growing pay has been rising in China. Foxconn expects to keep its huge customer but is negotiating to expand in India, where pay is much lower.

In emerging economies, many people move out of the agricultural sector and into manufacturing, where their productivity will be higher. As the economy becomes more mature, labour-saving investment increases and more people will move into the service sector. As education becomes more widespread, people acquire more skills. For a long time educated and trained people have been easier to find in Asia and Latin America than in Africa. This may change but perhaps not very soon.

Economic growth makes travel more affordable. Increasingly we live in a globalised labour market where people migrate to get jobs and employers look abroad for the best candidates.

Inorganic growth

Businesses that are looking to grow often choose the inorganic route, taking over businesses in foreign countries. This can be a quick way to reap economies of scale and acquire skilled staff. They may rationalise the new business by closing down parts of it or moving production from one location to another, seeking to make best possible use of all their assets.

Consumers have reaped many benefits from globalisation and technical change. Pay has risen for most, over the long term, but also, some prices have fallen or risen more slowly. The quality of many products has improved, giving better value for money. For example, cars used to require regular repairs and maintaining a car was not cheap. Nowadays those costs are much lower because cars are built to be more reliable.

For developed economies, there are downsides to global growth. Both shifting production to countries where labour costs are lower and the arrival of newly competitive imports can lead to redundancies. People with scarce skills simply move on to the next job, suffering little more than a period of nervousness. Those with obsolete skills or no skills at all may experience a permanent loss of income that is very serious. Some employees in emerging economies have received increased incomes but their working conditions may have deteriorated if they are doing very monotonous or risky work.

> **Think!**
> 1. Current trends suggest a need for individuals to acquire education and skills. How might this affect (a) businesses that are recruiting and (b) the pay and living standards of unskilled people?
> 2. What opportunities have current patterns of economic growth created for businesses? Think of two examples.

Indicators of growth: Gross Domestic Product (GDP)

It can be argued that GDP – gross domestic product – is not actually a very good measure of economic well-being. Specific issues relating to the money value of GDP as a whole include:

- *Inequality* – where this is significant, there may be a number of very wealthy people and a large number of people living in poverty. This may make the average per capita income appear quite comfortable, but ignore the existence of widespread poverty. Clearly national well-being would be greater if fewer people were suffering from very low incomes.

Measuring GDP

- *Exchange rates* make international comparisons difficult. We usually compare economic data from different countries by converting the figures to US dollars. But comparisons will change if exchange rates fluctuate. Using **purchasing power parity** (**PPP**) exchange rates helps somewhat with this by allowing for differences in prices.

- *The hidden economy* – sometimes paid work is not recorded or declared to the tax authorities; this is called the black economy. In the UK it is estimated to be 10% of GDP, in China 20% and in Sub-Saharan Africa, 50 – 60%

- *Home produced goods* – particularly in developing economies, many people rely on the food they produce themselves and this is not recorded as part of GDP. This happens very little in developed economies as we buy most food in shops from which farmers receive an income.

Additional problems arise because GDP figures do not measure important aspects of well-being such as the availability of health care and education, housing, and environmental regulation. Building a clear picture means studying both GDP and a range of other helpful indicators.

> **Purchasing power parity** (**PPP**) means that the data has been adjusted so that it allows for differing price levels in different economies. It uses exchange rates that give accurate comparisons of purchasing power.

Literacy

The literacy rate is the percentage of the population aged 15 and above who can read and write a short statement on their everyday lives. It is a key indicator of the economic situation: rising literacy rates lead to an improvement in the economy's human resources. There is a strong link between literacy and efficiency and growth. Educated workers are more likely to find better employment and improve their standard of living. As each person benefits, so too does the economy. This is why governments are keen to develop education provision. An increased literacy rate usually leads to decreasing population growth rates; resources can be better shared amongst fewer people.

Health

A country with a healthy population is more likely to grow and develop for a variety of reasons. Healthy workers are likely to be more productive. Diseases such as malaria and AIDS have a real impact on individuals, families and employment. Better health means fewer demands on the health care system; scarce government funds can be used to improve education or infrastructure, leading to more growth. Many big companies that operate in developing countries operate healthcare programmes for their workforce, partly for altruistic reasons but also to keep productivity high. Health is also linked to nutrition, so it is important to improve the quality and quantity of food available.

The Human Development Index (HDI)

The UN's Human Development Index (HDI) complements GDP data by providing additional information which allows much more subtle international comparisons. The HDI is a composite ranking based on Gross National Income (GNI)* per capita at purchasing power parity, together with life expectancy and years of schooling.

Some countries will get a higher ranking than their GNI would suggest because they have comparatively good health and education systems. Table 2 shows the HDI ranking and GNI for a range of developed, emerging and developing economies. The rankings are determined by the HDI figure on the right. High development countries identified here are all usually described as emerging economies, as are some in the medium development group.

Table 2: Human Development Index data, selected economies, 2014

World ranking and GNI* per capita at PPP	Country	HDI	World ranking and GNI* per capita at PPP	Country	HDI
Very High Development			**High Development**		
1 $65,000	Norway	.944	50 $22,000	Russia	.798
8 $53,000	USA	.915	62 $23,000	Malaysia	.779
14 $39,000	UK	.907	72 $19,000	Turkey	.761
15 $46,000	Korea	.898	74 $17,000	Mexico	.756
20 $37,000	Japan	.891	75 $15,000	Brazil	.755
22 $38,000	France	.888	90 $13,000	China	.727
Medium Development			**Low Development**		
110 $10,000	Indonesia	.684	142 $3,000	Kenya	.570
130 $5,000	India	.609	158 $5,000	Myanmar	.536
140 $4,000	Ghana	.579	180 $1,000	Mozambique	.416
142 $3,000	Bangladesh	.570	181 $2,000	Sierra Leone	.413

Source: UN Human Development Report 2015   *GNI is very close to GDP. The main difference is that it includes net income from abroad.

Other influences on well-being

The HDI does not tell us about the effects of inequality, the level of unemployment or underemployment, or housing quality. It does not tell us whether the country concerned has been devastated by wars or natural disasters that slow the development process. But it does provide much more information than the GDP figures alone.

Exam style question (Paper 3)

Infosys was started up in 1981 in Pune, India, by seven people with US$250 between them for working capital. They offered IT services to business. By 2014, sales revenue was $8.7 billion and there were 176,000 employees. The company has branches all over the world and reckons to be able to help make almost any business more efficient. It has world-class capability in the design of IT systems and finds tailor-made solutions to individual problems. Its customers can be anywhere – systems are designed to fit their precise needs. The programming will often be done in India; there Infosys can recruit highly trained IT specialists at comparatively low cost. Customers are typically in manufacturing, energy, transport, retailing, finance or healthcare. Of course, a business like this could not develop without the ability to communicate internationally, easily and cheaply.

Tata is a much older Indian company, founded in 1907. It's bigger too – sales revenue was $103 billion in 2014, a 6.7% increase on 2013. It has interests worldwide, spread across steel, cars, IT, communications, energy, hotels and tea. It bought several European companies, including Corus steel, Jaguar Land Rover and Tetley Tea. It is still run by the Tata family.

1. Jaguar Land Rover vehicles sell well in China. Explain possible reasons for this.   *(8 marks)*

2. Assess the strategies used by Infosys to develop its business.   *(10 marks)*

3. Assess possible reasons why India is still a poor country.   *(12 marks)*

4. Both Tata and Infosys locate much of their production activity in India.
   Evaluate the extent to which this may have contributed to their success.   *(20 marks)*

Chapter 2

International trade and business growth

Terms to revise: economies of scale (Theme 3), competitive advantage (Theme 1),

Trade

Trade has existed as long as the human race has been around. Our ancestors would swap goods between communities to benefit from each other's different skills and specialisations. Trade took place over longer and longer distances, eventually crossing borders and becoming international. Ancient civilisations such as the Egyptians, Greeks, and Romans all had extensive trading networks. In the Far East the Silk Road became a major channel for ideas and culture as well as unusual and exotic goods.

Discussion point
What are the incentives that lead people to trade?

Exports and imports

Globalisation

In the last century or so trade has really increased, particularly in the last few decades. Driven by a combination of technology, political and social change, international trade links have become closer than at any point in human history. Global flows of goods, services and capital are worth trillions of dollars every year. They continue to rise due to globalisation and the increasingly interconnected nature of modern trade.

All international trade can be classified as exports and imports, depending on its direction of travel. A good or service that enters a country from abroad is an import. When that country produces a product and then sells it in another country, that is an export. Sometimes it can be confusing to work out which is which. Tourism is a good example. An American family visiting the UK is classed as an export, while a UK family spending a holiday in Spain would be classed as an import. The trick is to 'follow the money': the American family will bring a flow of money into the UK from abroad; the UK family represents a flow of money from the UK into Spain and is therefore an import.

Example
Tourism is actually a valuable export for the UK economy. In 2014 the UK earned £21.7bn from foreign visitors. The UK is the eighth largest international tourism destination, ranked by both visitor numbers and visitor expenditure.

Invisible exports

Technically, tourism is a service. So foreign tourists in the UK are an **invisible export**. Other invisibles include transport (by sea or air), financial services (including insurance), legal and consultancy services, technical and design services, media services and education. A physical or tangible product is classed as **visible**. Visible exports include a huge range of products such as computers, cars, drinks, raw materials, food and clothing.

Visible imports

Visible imports and exports include manufactured products, raw materials and natural resources.

Invisible imports and exports include all kinds of services: for example, the best architects sell their services all over the world.

Think!
Identify three visible imports that you have bought recently and three invisible imports. Having trouble thinking of three? Maybe you have watched an American movie? Wouldn't some of the ticket money have gone to California?

The link between business specialisation and competitive advantage

Innovation

A very technical product

Strix started out making control mechanisms in the Isle of Man in 1982. It was always an innovative business. It had a lot to do with the introduction of cordless kettles. It manufactures the tiny kettle sensors that monitor the temperature of the water inside and tell the kettle to switch off when the water is boiling.

In 2009 Strix celebrated the sale of its 1 billionth sensor. One in five people in the world use Strix safety controls every day. The business has about two thirds of the world market in kettle sensors. Sales in 2014 were worth over £100 million.

950 people are employed worldwide. The really technical part of the production process happens close to the head office in Ronaldsway, Isle of Man. These components are then shipped out to Guangzhou in China for assembly, along with other parts. Strix attributes its success to the very high quality of the people and the teamwork in its multicultural workforce.

Components

Strix is part of a trend whereby some small businesses specialise in highly technical devices that are usually hidden inside much larger products, greatly improving their functionality. Intel is the biggest example, manufacturing micro-chips. These component products become part of a supply chain involving many businesses.

Questions

1. Can you think of any other businesses that have a very specialised product?

2. Why does it make sense to specialise in designing and manufacturing a small range of tiny products that consumers never see?

3. What is it about Strix that has enabled it to develop such a large market?

Specialisation

What happens when people get together to produce something? They don't all do the same things, each starting from scratch and producing a finished product. There is a division of labour. Each individual plays a part in the production process. With practice, each gets better at their own task. Construction projects involve people with many different skills – crane drivers, ironworkers, scaffolders and pipefitters at first, with carpenters, electricians and plumbers coming later. There will be other specialists too, e.g. structural engineers, designers and accountants. Having the right skills around saves a lot of time and allows small teams to achieve high output levels.

**Division
of labour**

⚠ WATCH OUT!

Make sure you understand economies of scale: reductions in average costs brought about by expanding output. It helps businesses to cut prices and enlarge their markets and can give them a competitive advantage.

**Competitive
advantage**

> The **division of labour** involves organising employees so that individuals specialise in one part of the production process. As they become quicker and more proficient at specific tasks, output increases.
>
> **Specialisation** refers to the process by which individuals, businesses and economies concentrate on creating and selling those goods and services that they produce most efficiently and cost effectively.

Specialisation means that people make the most of their skills by concentrating on what they do best. As a skilled person produces more, output per head rises. This only works when people or economies are in a position to trade their output for things they need but do not produce.

When you start to think about international trade, you see at once that economies become specialised, each producing the things they are best placed to produce. Their advantages may include natural resources, abundant land, cheap labour, scarce skills, technical know-how, a favourable climate, beautiful scenery, a deep-water port, a university active in scientific research or accessible sources of finance.

Specialisation

A country like the UK could grow bananas but it would take a huge amount of energy and expenditure to overcome the difficulties of producing such a crop in our climate. It is far more efficient to leave the banana growing to countries that do have the right climate, concentrate on what we do best and then trade to get our bananas. The UK is probably best known for specialising in financial services although we do of course produce many other goods and services.

Specialisation allows a country to build up expertise as well as producing particular goods or services at a lower cost. Fewer resources are used and by trading with a country in a similar position global output increases and uses resources more efficiently. Economists call this the Theory of Comparative Advantage, an idea first explained by David Ricardo (1772-1823). It is not part of this particular specification but in simple terms it says that if a country specialises in what it is comparatively best at doing (or comparatively least bad at doing) and then trades, economic growth will occur. This idea lies behind the wealth generated

WTO

by trade. It is why the World Trade Organisation (WTO) is so keen to break down trade barriers and encourage developing nations, in particular, to trade and grow. It pays to do what you do best, even if others can do it even better. It always pays to specialise and trade.

Developing a competitive advantage

Michael Porter developed the idea of competitive advantage. Put simply, it means the advantage that specific businesses have in terms of keen prices, quality, reliability, value for money or just attractiveness. Specialisation also gives a competitive advantage to a whole economy. Sometimes, the nature of an economy's natural resources determines its competitive advantage. Oil, minerals and productive farmland are obvious areas of specialisation for some. Others may exploit technical skills or scientific knowledge and research. All economies have a competitive advantage in certain products and services, those that they can produce most efficiently, giving the best value for money. The economies with a strong competitive advantage use their business dynamism to become flexible, adapting to current trends, designing and investing in the products for which there is strong demand.

Example
Japan has few valuable natural resources. So it has specialised in high quality, reliable manufactures, using its technical expertise and setting high standards.

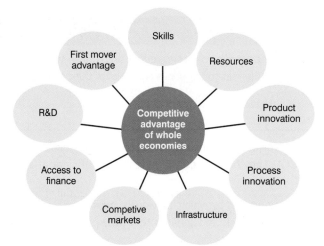

Economies of scale

When competitive businesses specialise, they can expand output, reap economies of scale, selling in new markets and contributing to economic growth by cutting costs and unit prices. For some, the increase in sales may bring higher profits. Less efficient businesses may just survive by adopting new strategies. They

Globalisation has made economies much more interdependent.

may discontinue some production lines because they cannot find a way to develop a competitive advantage. The least efficient will close down altogether or perhaps be taken over by stronger companies.

Adapting to change

Example
In the UK, most civilian shipbuilding yards closed down in the 1970s and 80s, as South Korea became more and more competitive. None of the UK shipbuilders' customers wanted to pay UK prices. But other UK businesses had no difficulty in expanding sales of office equipment, aerospace products, Scotch whisky and legal and education services (among other things).

Exploiting competitive advantage

Globalisation has made economies much more interdependent. Specialisation means that many needs will be met by imports. Gradually the domestic industries that supplied those needs will become redundant and close down. The UK used to have many coal mines, steel works and shipyards. Most of these have gone as it is cheaper to import our needs from those economies that have successfully specialised in those areas. These trends are positive for the majority of people as newer industries in which we do have a competitive advantage have grown in size. (Think of aerospace – Airbus and Rolls Royce's aero engines.) However, this change does involve lost jobs. Skilled people easily find work in expanding businesses or self-employment but people with limited or obsolete skills may experience significant income losses.

Show your understanding
Identify two more UK businesses that have grown in size and become significant exporters. Explain where their competitive advantages lie. (These businesses need not necessarily be British-owned.)

Foreign direct investment (FDI)

Foreign direct investment (FDI) is a flow of investment from one country to another. It occurs when businesses set up factories or other kinds of production or distribution facilities in other countries. Much FDI flows from one developed country to another, usually to expand into new markets. Their potentially profitable markets attract investment from many foreign businesses.

Increasingly, FDI is flowing into emerging economies too, as businesses seek locations with lower wage rates. Moving production to countries with lower input costs is known as **offshoring**. Some FDI is directed towards production for local markets.

Offshoring

> **FDI** occurs when companies with their head office in one country, set up factories or offices or distribution outlets in another country. The investment is in production facilities or warehousing or other facilities on the ground, not in loans to local businesses.
>
> **Offshoring** means locating all or part of the production process in a foreign economy, usually where production costs are lower. It can mean getting foreign businesses to supply the products. It also applies to businesses that are making a direct investment in a low-cost location. They may build and run a factory or office block or set up a call centre.

Many businesses have embraced globalisation. Offshoring, setting up production facilities where labour costs are relatively low, increases profitability. FDI has been a significant driving force in the growth of trade. Investment flows are still highest between the developed economies, where **multinational corporations** (**MNCs**) can see prospects of profit. FDI is also significant where MNCs seek to invest in emerging economies to cut labour costs. War-torn and very poor countries, the developing economies, attract very little FDI. generally have very low incomes, cheap labour but little capital investment. Lack of infrastructure (roads, ports etc.), education and training facilities may make them unattractive to investors.

MNCs

> **Multinational corporations** (**MNCs**) are businesses which operate or have assets in more than one country.

FDI

Most governments welcome FDI. It creates jobs, sometimes in regions which badly need them. If the objective is to be close to the market, it may reduce imports. If it is to export, then the new activities will serve a wider market. The UK government facilitated the FDI that came with Nissan and Toyota manufacturing in the UK. The main motive for these Japanese companies was to produce inside the EU, thus avoiding import duties.

Nissan in North-East England

Trying to avoid tariffs (see pages 14-15) and cut delivery costs in the EU, Nissan chose to build its car plant near Sunderland. There were government incentives. Also, the area had a rich industrial heritage and a strong reputation for engineering skills, backed up by specialist colleges and universities. It had access to two deep water ports.

A major manufacturer draws many other firms to the area to supply it with components. These new businesses now supply Ford, Vauxhall and others, as well as Nissan.

Since 1986, Nissan has invested over £2.5 billion in the area. It is estimated that it employs 5,000 people directly and another 15,000 are employed indirectly, supplying components. This might change when the UK leaves the EU.

Questions

1. Why was the UK government willing to offer incentives to Nissan?

2. Explain why other businesses such as the component suppliers have moved into the area.

3. Assess the relative importance of the factors that may have led to Nissan choosing the Sunderland site.

Investing abroad to achieve growth

FDI goes out as well as in. There are many reasons for businesses to invest abroad but the foremost are those key objectives, profit and sales. FDI facilitates trade and is changing in many ways, quite rapidly.

Outsourcing

- FDI is often associated with a global **supply chain**, as MNCs look to **outsource** the most labour intensive parts of their production process from other countries. Strix is a good example. Very technical processes are located in the Isle of Man whilst assembly takes place in China.

- FDI can cut production costs: Taiwanese businesses have built factories in China, such as Foxconn, that produce Apple computers using low-paid labour. This helps to explain the impressive profitability of Apple.

- Some emerging countries are investing abroad. China's foreign investment is growing fast; this may continue. In Africa, the Chinese government hopes its investments will secure long-term supplies of natural resources.

- Many companies want access to the Chinese market of 1.37 billion people with growing incomes. In some cases, FDI is aimed at cutting costs by producing close to the market. A US producer of air conditioners did well by both producing and selling in China.

- Saturated domestic markets encourage many businesses to expand into other economies: Tesco and M&S have targeted millions of potential customers in a range of different countries. Tesco has been very successful in Poland and South Korea but much less so in China and the USA.

- Suppliers of luxury goods have developed profitable markets in both developed and emerging economies where there are growing numbers of wealthy people – for example, Burberry, Jaguar Land Rover, Louis Vuitton and many others. But many other businesses find markets abroad – such as IKEA and Primark, which is expanding into the USA.

Supply chains

> A **supply chain** is the sequence of processes by which many independent suppliers contribute to the production of the finished product. Different businesses may be involved in production of raw materials, component parts and some services e.g. design, testing and packaging.
>
> **Outsourcing** means shifting all or part of the production process to other businesses in order to reduce input costs.

FDI is all about capital investments flowing between one economy and another. It is not just for the big MNCs – smaller firms find it useful and profitable too. Foreign investors may share know-how and technologies with their overseas partners. FDI has been very beneficial in creating jobs and opening up new markets, enhancing prosperity.

Exam style question

India was the highest ranked country by capital investment in 2015, with $63bn-worth of FDI projects announced. It replaced China as the top destination for FDI, following a year of high-value project announcements, specifically across the coal, oil, natural gas and renewable energy sectors.

Much of this increase is due to the 'Make in India' campaign launched by the Indian Government in 2014. There has been an ongoing series of reforms since 2013 to improve the ease of doing business (see page 44). This campaign and the increase in FDI has raised FDI job creation from 116,000 new jobs in 2013 to 225,000 in 2015 – the fastest annual FDI-based employment growth in the world.

1. Why would the Indian Government be so keen to attract FDI?   *(4 marks)*

2. Explain two possible reasons why India is such a popular target for FDI.   *(6 marks)*

3. Assess the impact on Indian businesses of increased levels of FDI.   *(12 marks)*

Chapter 3
Factors contributing to increased globalisation

Protectionism

Terms to revise: market power (Theme 3)

Protectionism

After World War II it was clear that tariffs (taxes placed on imports) made products dearer for consumers and also sheltered businesses that were inefficient compared to overseas competitors. While the United Nations was being set up, governments worked together to create the General Agreement on Tariffs and Trade (GATT) which later became the World Trade Organisation (WTO).

Every few years, the member countries met to discuss reductions in tariffs and other import controls. They sought to make imported products cheaper and markets more competitive, helping to raise standards of living.

Discussion points

What are the advantages and disadvantages of tariffs (import duties)? Who would benefit from lower tariffs?

Trade liberalisation

Trade barriers include any measure that prevents or slows down the process of trade. Many countries have in the past used trade barriers to protect their own industries from foreign competition. This is called **protectionism**; there is more on this in Chapter 4. As globalisation has increased, trade barriers have been reduced via **trade liberalisation**. Where there are fewer import controls, businesses with good products can export more. World trade in manufactured products has become very much freer.

> **Protectionism** refers to the way in which governments may control imports so that domestic producers face less competition. Reduced imports enable them to charge more even if their product is of a lower quality.
>
> **Trade liberalisation** refers to the process of limiting and reducing barriers to trade so that the economies involved move closer to free trade, (i.e. no trade barriers at all).

Trade barriers

Trade liberalisation means that buyers have much more choice about where they obtain the products they want. Many businesses find it harder to compete but the ones that do well have access to far larger markets. They are able to operate more efficiently than do their weaker competitors and can exploit economies of scale. Struggling businesses may end in closing down or diversifying. Others adapt, learning how to cut costs.

Tariffs

Quotas

Trade barriers can be used by governments to protect inefficient industries. **Tariffs** are taxes that increase the prices of imports; they allow inefficient industries to sell at prices above the world market level. **Quotas** put a limit on the level of imports of specific products. By increasing competition, trade liberalisation keeps prices down, greatly benefiting consumers. Vested interests often try to get governments to enact trade protection measures that help them to stay alive but this does lead to slower economic growth. (In 2015-16 steel manufacturers in the EU wanted their governments to raise tariffs to keep out cheap Chinese imports. This could help the steelmakers to survive but would raise steel prices.)

By increasing competition, trade liberalisation keeps prices down, greatly benefiting consumers.

> **Trade barriers** make trade more difficult. **Tariffs** put a tax on imports. **Quotas** allow only a limited quantity of imports of certain specific products. All trade barriers reduce the amount of trade taking place.

Think!
Think about how trade liberalisation has affected you personally. How would your clothing purchases be different if there had been less trade liberalisation and higher tariffs on clothing?

Trade liberalisation

Trade liberalisation started in the 1950s but it really took off with the Uruguay Round of negotiations in the early 1990s. The international agreement reduced tariffs and other trade barriers on manufactures, enabling exporters everywhere to expand and grow. Having greatly increased the international trade in manufactures, many governments wanted to encourage increased trade in agricultural products and in services. The new Doha Round of negotiations was launched in 2001. However, liberalising trade in agricultural products proved to be much more difficult than liberalising trade in manufactures. In 2007-8 the Doha negotiations slowed to a halt.

Meantime, discussion had begun on the TPP, the Trans-Pacific Partnership. This agreement was finalised by 12 countries around the Pacific rim early in 2016 but it was not immediately approved by the US Congress. At the time of writing it is not clear whether the next President of the USA will press for it to be implemented.

Another trade negotiation, the Transatlantic Trade and Investment Partnership (TTIP), involves the US, the EU and a number of other economies from around the Atlantic Ocean. It seeks to reduce regulatory barriers to trade, such as food safety regulation, environmental legislation and banking regulations. These negotiations could eventually lead to all the usual benefits of trade: higher real incomes, lower prices and more choice. The US proposals for 'regulatory co-operation', similar to EU harmonisation arrangements, could standardise products and so cut prices, perhaps improving quality.

Will TPP and TTIP happen?

Trade negotiations

These trade negotiations have been very controversial. Many people in Europe are worried that TTIP might open up Europe's public health, education and water services to competition from US companies. Many believe that TTIP would give the MNCs far too much market power.

Trade liberalisation and globalisation have led to some businesses growing very large indeed. Some have very substantial market power. (The impact of multinational corporations (MNCs) is discussed in more detail in Chapters 14 and 16.) Given that many MNCs are economically more powerful than many individual economies, it is easy to see how they might dominate global markets.

Find out
As this book is being written, there is great uncertainty in the global economy. Find out what happened to the TPP and TTIP after the 2016 US presidential elections. Will it be possible to reap additional benefits from freer trade? Identify possible gainers and losers from this process.

Political change

China

Until about 1980, China was relatively isolated from the rest of the world; there was very little trade. Then, slowly at first, the Chinese Communist government moved towards a strategy of collaboration with foreign businesses and governments. At that time, the majority of people in China were still living in the countryside and getting a limited income from farming. Then more and more moved to the cities to work in the growing manufacturing sector. Chinese businesses benefited from access to new technologies that were being developed outside China and productivity rose. After 1980, China's trade developed very rapidly and led to significantly higher standards of living for many Chinese people. Over time, wage rates in China have risen so some businesses are now offshoring production in other countries with cheaper labour, such as Vietnam.

Figure 1: UK exports, imports and trade balance with China, 2004 to 2014

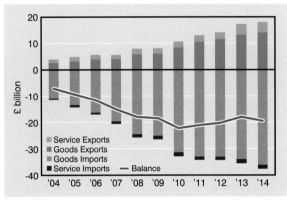

Source: ONS

The importance of China to the UK economy has grown steadily and it is now the UK's second largest import partner after the USA. 7% of UK imports come from China. UK exports to China have grown more slowly.

The USSR, Union of Soviet Socialist Republics, lasted from 1917 until 1989. There was always some trade with western economies, but not much. In 1989 the USSR split; Russia remained by far the largest economy alongside a number of independent governments, such as Kazakhstan, Ukraine, Belarus and others. International trade developed by degrees and economic growth improved standards of living over time, though not at the same pace as in China. Russia uses the revenues from its oil and gas exports to finance imports. Most of Russia's energy exports go to neighbouring and EU economies.

Russia

The EU

The breakup of the Soviet Union freed East European countries to join the EU. The unification of East and West Germany made Germany by far the largest economy in the EU. These events have had powerful effects on the world economy, leading to many structural changes. Many opportunities have opened up, especially for businesses that benefited from reduced labour costs. Within the EU, many member countries relocated all or part of their production processes to the new member countries where both land and labour are cheaper.

Despite short-run job losses resulting from shifting patterns of production, many economies including the UK have managed to keep unemployment relatively low, except of course during the financial crisis (2008-9) and the subsequent recession.

> **Think!**
> Explain in your own words how political changes have affected the global economy.

Transport and communication

**Communica-
tion**

Falling costs of transport and communication have hastened globalisation. Advances in technology have made it much easier to co-ordinate business operations around the world. Conference calls between several countries can be conducted on mobile phones. Broadband facilitates complex information exchanges. Cheaper air travel makes it easier to negotiate complex deals. Businesses can make quick decisions, reacting swiftly to changes in dynamic markets and seizing opportunities ahead of the competition. Offshoring and outsourcing became much easier.

Table 1: Index of changes in transport and communications costs over the period 1930-2004

	1930	1950	1960	1970	1990	2004
Air transport cost per passenger mile	100	44	56	24	16	12
Cost of a 3 minute telephone call from London to New York	100	22	19	13	14	<1

Source: Globalisation and the changing UK economy, Department for Business, Enterprise and Regulatory Reform 2008, (now known as Department for Business, Energy & Industrial Strategy). It covers the period when the most rapid changes took place but there has been some continuing progress. 100 represents the starting prices in 1930. See page 107 for more on index numbers.

These developments cut the costs of international trade.

**Containerisa-
tion**

● A single container can be used to take goods by road or rail to the docks, be lifted onto container ships by cranes, and carry on similarly at the other end until it reaches the final market. Containerisation has

Transport

revolutionised global trade, cutting costs and reducing transit times. It has eliminated much labour intensive loading and unloading of cargoes.

● Air freight prices have fallen far enough for perishable products to be exported. Other products have high value in relation to their bulk. Speed reduces the need for finance to cover production costs until the sales revenue comes in. Automated freight handling at airports helped too.

● Computerised data handling made it easier and cheaper to keep track of goods in transit.

Show your understanding

In 1961, before containers were used, ocean freight costs accounted for 12 percent of the value of US exports and 10 percent of the value of US imports. At the time the average US import tariff was 7 percent.

To what extent did containerisation affect businesses and their customers?

Increased significance of global (transnational) companies

Trans-nationals

Transnational companies (TNCs) are the same as multinational companies (MNCs) and are inextricably linked with globalisation. TNCs are both a cause and consequence of globalisation.

A large multinational

Walmart is an American multinational corporation and retailer. It is the world's largest company by revenue and the biggest private employer in the world with 2.2 million employees. In 2016 it had 11,545 stores and clubs in 28 countries, under a total of 63 different names, such as ASDA in the UK. Founded by Sam Walton in 1962 it is still owned and controlled by the Walton family.

A small multinational

Innovia Films is a leading producer of speciality polypropylene and cellulose films for packaging and labels. It supplies the film used to make the new 'plastic' bank notes for the UK. The company's head office is in Wigton in Cumbria.

Production is based on sites in America, Europe and Asia with sales offices throughout Europe and agents and distributors across the globe. With a turnover of over $595 million, the business employs some 1,400 people worldwide.

Questions
1. What advantages are there for businesses that have activities in a range of different countries?

2. How are host countries likely to be affected when foreign owned businesses locate there?

Multi-nationals

Multinational corporations (MNCs) are sometimes described as transnational corporations (TNCs) or multinational enterprises (MNEs). Such companies have offices or factories in different countries and usually have a centralised head office where they co-ordinate global management. The United Nations calculates that there are over 77,000 MNCs.

MNCs are nothing new. Early examples include the British East India Company in 1600, but they really began to develop early in the 20th century and proliferated after World War II. In recent years there has been a surge in the growth of MNCs. The spread of globalisation, the breaking down of trade barriers, the emergence of new markets, the liberalisation of existing markets and advances in information technology have all contributed to this.

They can be very large organisations with turnover exceeding the GDP of many countries. Inevitably this gives them great power and influence. Many MNCs have been accused of abusing their position and have attracted great criticism of their actions. But not all MNCs are large powerful corporations; many are small scale, like Innovia in the case study above.

● To their opponents, MNCs represent everything that is bad about global trade and globalisation. Their critics portray them as bullies, using their power to exploit workers and natural resources with scant regard for the economic or environmental well-being of any country or community.

● Their supporters see multinationals as a triumph for global capitalism, bringing employment and new technologies to poorer countries, driving up incomes and aiding development. In return, many consumers get cheaper goods.

Both viewpoints have some foundation in reality. The truth perhaps lies somewhere between the two. MNCs are examined in more detail in Chapters 14-16.

> Distrust of MNCs is nothing new. In a letter written in 1864, President Abraham Lincoln of the USA wrote… *"I see in the near future a crisis approaching that unnerves me and causes me to tremble for the safety of my country… corporations have been enthroned and an era of corruption in high places will follow, and the money power of the country will endeavor to prolong its reign by working upon the prejudices of the people until all wealth is aggregated in a few hands and the Republic is destroyed."*

In the past the largest MNCs were American, Japanese or European. But as globalisation has fostered the growth of economies such as India and China, they too now have large MNCs which are growing rapidly.

Asian MNCs

● Tata, the Indian conglomerate, has operations in over 85 countries across six continents and earns more than half its income outside India.

● State Grid is now the world's second largest business by revenue and China's biggest company. It is a giant utility company and enjoys monopoly status in China. Recently it has been investing heavily in alternative energy sources.

● One third of all cigarettes are smoked in China. The Chinese State Tobacco Company, the world's biggest tobacco company, is planning to expand into South America and Eastern Europe.

Table 2 shows the top global companies in 2016 as compiled by *Fortune* magazine. It is very likely that the biggest MNCs of the future will be Chinese or Indian and that they will come to dominate the global economy. If that seems doubtful, it is worth remembering that not so long ago, it seemed unlikely that a Finnish producer of rubber boots would go on to dominate the global market for mobile phones and that Nokia, in turn, would be overtaken by Samsung, a Korean chip maker.

Table 2: The top 10 MNCs by sales revenue, 2015

Big business

Rank	Company	Revenue ($ millions)
1	Walmart	482,130
2	State grid	329,601
3	China National Petroleum	299, 271
4	Sinopec	294,344
5	Royal Dutch Shell	272,156
6	Exxon Mobil	246,204
7	Volkswagen	236,600
8	Toyota	236,592
9	Apple	233,715
10	BP	225,982

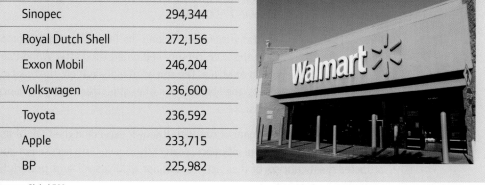

Source: Fortune, Global 500

Increased investment flows (FDI)

Many bigger businesses don't just want to export: they want to invest in new markets. Much FDI goes to developed or fast growing emerging economies so that companies can produce close to their markets. Many poor countries are not attractive to foreign investors; it may not be easy to do business there. Setting up a new project may be costly and offer limited profits. However, poorer countries are gradually attracting a little more FDI now. Table 3 shows the impact of FDI on developed, emerging and developing economies. India began trying hard to attract more FDI in 2014 and as of 2016, seems to be succeeding.

FDI destinations

Table 3: FDI, net inflows as % of GDP, 2011-14 and US$ billions in 2014

Economy	2011	2012	2013	2014	US$ bn, 2014
USA	1.7	1.4	1.3	0.8	131.8
UK	1.0	1.8	1.7	1.5	45.5
Japan	0.0	0.0	0.2	0.2	9.1
Germany	2.6	1.5	1.6	0.3	8.4
Brazil	2.7	3.2	3.4	4.1	1.5
China PRC	3.7	2.9	3.1	2.8	289.1
Russia	2.9	2.5	3.3	1.2	22.9
India	2.0	1.3	1.5	1.7	33.9
Uganda	4.4	5.2	4.4	4.2	1.1

Source: World Bank

The Nissan story (page 12) illustrates the reasons why most governments encourage FDI. Investment creates jobs and enhances prosperity. Many governments offer incentives for investors. Some, such as Ireland, keep their business tax rates low; this has proved to be a powerful incentive.

Inter-dependence

The UN's latest UNCTAD report (World Investment Report 2016) shows that in 2015 world investment flows jumped by 38% to $1.76 trillion, their highest level since the global economic and financial crisis of 2008–2009. Inward flows to developed economies reached $962bn while inward flows to developing economies reached a new high of $765bn. Increasing investment flows extend the reach of globalisation, increasing the interdependence of trading economies and the amount of trade that takes place. Most governments want to encourage the growth of trade. They generally recognise the need to collaborate with other governments in order to ensure economic growth.

Migration (within and between economies)

International trade enhances the forces of competition. When it becomes possible to import products that were previously unobtainable or very costly, consumers get to enjoy things that they could not previously afford. The people who produced the imports usually get higher wages than they did previously. Many people become better off. There will be structural change – some business will grow while others will shrink or close down.

Structural change

There are gainers and losers in this process. People who work in businesses that are unable to make a profit will lose their jobs. But an efficient economy needs skilled people. People who worked in agriculture migrate to urban centres and many learn new skills. Gradually their incomes improve to the point where they can travel further in search of the best (or sometimes any) job.

Employers are always on the lookout for people who will work for less than those they are already employing. Both employers and job seekers find they have incentives that lead to increased migration. So as well as increased trade, economic development leads to increased migration both within and between individual economies.

Many British people have moved to southeast England to find good jobs.

Think!

For some people, the labour market is now international. French bankers come to work in the City of London. Chinese people growing up on farms are likely to migrate to Chinese manufacturing centres. Many British people have moved to southeast England to find good jobs. People will often migrate to find work. How does migration affect employers and individuals?

Growth of the global labour force

Global labour markets

As economies prosper, education and training improves and individuals develop higher-level skills and capabilities. Migration is easier for people with skills and qualifications. Many MNCs are able to recruit in a global labour market. For example, there is an international shortage of people with engineering skills. Many businesses in developed economies find that recruiting abroad is cheaper than running their own training programmes. This helps them to grow and stay profitable.

As much as developed economies benefit from recruiting abroad, the economies that have net migration (more people moving out than moving in) may find that they are losing people with scarce skills. In 2016, just after the EU referendum, a Polish government official said on UK TV "*you have taken our best people.*" This is commonly known as a brain drain. This is not a new phenomenon – British scientists and teachers have been going abroad to work for many years. Many scientists moved to the USA, where more money is available for research.

Example

Carlos Ghosn

The CEO and Chair of Renault and Nissan is a French-Lebanese born in Brazil. Born in 1954, he was educated in France and worked both there and in Brazil. He is fluent in four languages. By 2004, surveys showed that he was the third most respected business leader in the world. In the 1990s Renault was struggling. Ghosn set about a radical restructuring of the company and brought it back to profitability. By the end of the decade he was known as 'Le Cost Killer'. He went on to turn around Nissan, which in 1999 was nearly bankrupt. An aggressive downsizing process set Nissan on its feet again and Ghosn became known in Japan as 'Mr Fix It'. Later he was asked to head first General Motors and then Ford, but he has stayed with the Renault-Nissan Alliance. He is trying hard to develop the world's first affordable electric car.

Globalisation and pay

Rates of pay can be affected by globalisation. Effectively many employees are competing in a global labour market. Trade unions that manage to negotiate higher pay may find that redundancies follow as the business becomes more automated. If this doesn't make the business profitable then the next step may be offshoring and many more redundancies. Across the developed world rates of pay for unskilled people have stagnated. The outcomes of offshoring include:

● a rise in incomes in the emerging economies; people there gain more spending power and demand for imports from developed economies increases

● many goods (especially clothing) become relatively cheaper in the developed economies, which are importing them from the emerging economies

● businesses in the developed economies export more and concentrate on new product development, creating new jobs

● as all economies prosper, education and training helps to increase skill levels and productivity.

Adapting to globalisation contributes to economic growth. The process of globalisation involves significant structural change as it lifts incomes.

Structural change

Table 4: Then and now

	1800	2015
Global population	c.1bn	> 7bn
% urbanisation	c.3%	54%
Main work	c.85% agriculture	70% services*
World trade/GDP	c.3%	c.30%

Source: World Bank   *In developed economies

There are three stages in the development process. Developing economies depend heavily on agriculture; manufacturing develops in emerging economies and developed economies are dominated by the production of services. As economies grow richer they invest in physical capital (machinery and infrastructure) and human capital (skills and abilities). Many unskilled jobs become mechanised and then automated. Skill shortages are common as development brings change and the labour force takes time to adjust.

Urbanisation

Urbanisation, with more people moving from agriculture to manufacturing, raises productivity. China's urbanisation has been the fastest in human history. In 1950, 13% of China's population lived in cities. By 2010, the urban share of the population had grown to 45%; it is projected to reach 60% by 2030. Shanghai, with more than 23 million people, is currently the largest and wealthiest city in China. Around 500m Chinese people have moved out of poverty.

Figure 2 (overleaf) shows how structural changes led to growth in the UK service sector. In 1841 the industrial revolution was largely complete. The decline in the proportion of manufacturing employment is higher in the UK than in most developed economies, partly because of the growth in financial services. The fall in employment in the energy sector reflects the rapid decline in coal mining.

Agriculture in developing economies uses labour intensive methods with little capital or fertiliser and limited irrigation. If some workers move to towns, incomes improve, new methods are adopted and yields rise.

Rising incomes

Globally, the proportion of people living in towns grew from 30% in 1930 to 54% in 2014. By 2030, an estimated 60% will be in urban areas. 1980 estimates of the proportion of Chinese people living in poverty varied between 60% and 81%, depending on the definition used. The 2014 United Nations estimate of poverty in China was 11.8%, predominantly found in rural areas.

Structural change

Figure 2: Employment by sector, UK, 1841-2011, % of labour force employed by sector

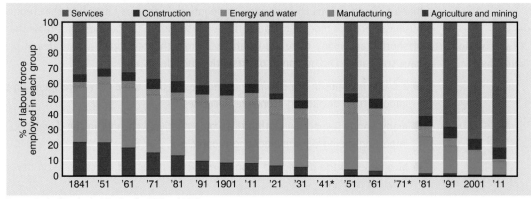

Source: Bank of England   *No data for 1941 and 1971

> **Think!**
>
> What long terms consequences would you expect from widespread urbanisation and growing manufacturing sectors in emerging economies over the next 10 years? What opportunities might this open up for businesses?

The knowledge economy

In developed, mature, economies around 70% of the workforce will be in the service sector. Production will be capital intensive. Australia's mineral mining, for example, employs relatively few people and is capital intensive. Production involves mechanisation, automation and little human labour. Technological advances play an important role. The knowledge economy and service industries provide the most jobs. Structural change involves creative destruction. Some businesses and some whole industries decline while new opportunities are developing. New industries flourish and the new jobs are very different from the old ones.

> The **knowledge economy** describes how knowledge, skills and innovative technology drive economic activity and create a competitive advantage.
>
> **Creative destruction** refers to the way in which competitive advantage shifts away from existing businesses while new, innovative, products and production processes develop and the businesses involved grow in size and importance.

Retraining

Structural change involves retraining and life-time learning as employers' needs change. People who are made redundant from declining industries need help to become more mobile and adaptable. Training schemes are needed to reduce skill shortages. Adapting to structural change is much easier if the labour market is fairly flexible.

Investment in robots in manufacturing processes is already reducing global job opportunities. This trend may soon extend into the service sector. This could make for a very different kind of structural change over the coming years.

Slowing growth

In late 2016 there were signs that the recent slow-down in international trade growth was continuing. During 2016, estimated trade growth for the year fell from 2.8% to 1.7%. Figure 2 on page 40 shows that since 2010, international trade as a percentage of global GDP has been stable. More on this on page 107.

> **Exam style question**
>
> Evaluate the impact of globalisation on business strategies.   *(20 marks)*

Chapter 4

Protectionism

Tariffs

Tariffs on shoes and textiles

Shoemakers in the EU have campaigned vigorously to block imports of cheap trainers from Vietnam and China. They have not been very successful and millions of consumers are happy about that. But within the EU there are a number of businesses that can produce competitive clothing and footwear items. Ricosta, a fashion shoe manufacturer based in Germany, with 800 employees in Germany, Hungary, Poland and Romania, exports two million pairs of shoes a year, but only 10,000 to the USA.

US tariffs (import duties) on manufactures from the EU are generally around 3% – in line with global trade liberalisation agreements. But for some products such as cars, clothing and footwear, import duties are much higher, going up to 40% on some fashion items.

Italian shoemakers point out that non-tariff barriers create problems too. For example, complex paperwork and labeling requirements make it harder to export to US markets. They warn that EU exporters will have to put more effort into finding lawyers, agents and distributors in the US who will help them to get over the barriers.

UK negotiators have complained about the effects of US tariffs on labels like Burberry and Paul Smith. Overcoats can face 28% tariffs.

TTIP could change all this.

Discussion points

Who gains from tariffs and non-tariff barriers? Who loses? Name at least two of each, both gainers and losers.

Standards of living

The whole point of trade is to get what you want from the supplier whose products provide the best value for money. Cheap imports are very pleasing – they make our incomes go further and often raise standards of living. When we can get the things we have to have at reasonable prices, we have more money left over to spend on other things – for example, tickets for football matches, theatres and cinemas.

Protectionism – how tariffs work

When businesses, jobs and incomes are threatened, it is very tempting for governments to try to protect sectors that are vulnerable to competition from abroad. The obvious way to do this is to control imports. This can be done using tariffs or quotas or a combination of measures. These are the elements of protectionism, which can be used to keep businesses going and preserve jobs when competition is a problem.

Tariffs are usually intended to protect sales of domestic products from competitive imported substitutes. The substitute may or may not be a good one. But if it is, as with the EU-made fashion shoes in the case study, then demand will be price elastic. So when prices rise to cover the cost of the tariff, imports will fall substantially. The domestic producer will sell more and may be able to raise prices and increase profits. Their shareholders will be happy. Figure 1 (overleaf) shows what happens.

Figure 1: Tariffs on products that have elastic demand

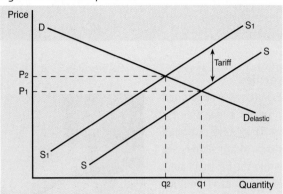

Tariffs can be used in a range of circumstances.

Tariffs affect prices

● They can protect specific industries or sectors from foreign competition. Many developed countries want to protect their agricultural sectors. The EU's Common Agricultural Policy (CAP) protects farmers; for some products it is very restrictive indeed. For example cane sugar can be produced more cheaply than sugar made from sugar beet. So sugar prices within the EU are often well above world prices. Higher prices for many food products mean that consumers' real incomes are reduced. On the other hand, EU farm incomes are kept high enough to keep farmers in business.

● Tariffs raise tax revenue: if demand for the relevant import is inelastic, people will continue to buy it even though the price is higher; the government will collect taxes that can be used to help fund public expenditure.

Dumping

● Tariffs can be used to deter **dumping**. This occurs when the exporter is selling the product at a price below the cost of production. Consumers are often pleased to be able to get very cheap imports but a business that is competing with dumped imports will usually feel very aggrieved. The WTO permits anti-dumping duties under certain circumstances, in order to deter unfair competition.

Infant industries

● The **infant industry** argument holds that if small industries, those that are just getting started, are protected for a while, they may in time become more expert and reap economies of scale, and so be able to compete effectively without protection. This is an argument for temporary measures.

> **Dumping** means exporting at a price that is less than the true cost of production.
>
> **Infant industries** are those with some prospect of profitability in the long run, provided they are given some protection in the short run while they get started.

When governments use import controls to protect many of their domestic producers, they are said to be adopting inward-looking policies. On the whole, these have not been successful except in isolated instances. The snag with import controls generally is that although they do reduce imports, they also annoy the exporter. If that leads to retaliation, it may mean that jobs are lost in exporting industries.

> **Show your understanding**
> Why does public opinion sometimes support the use of import controls?
> Why do governments retaliate when their exports are subject to import controls?

Tariffs and elasticity

Price elasticity of demand

When tariffs cause prices to rise, demand may be price inelastic (i.e. substitutes are either unavailable or inferior). That means that many customers will simply buy the imported item anyway and pay the higher price. This leaves them with less money to spend on other things. Tariffs on cars or video games may help domestic manufacturers to increase sales revenue – the protection means they can charge a higher price and probably sell more too. Businesses, their employees and their shareholders will be happy. But if that leads to people having less money to spend on meals out, restaurant owners and their employees will be unhappy.

Tariffs have a range of consequences that may not be obvious when they are introduced:

Import prices

● Consumers have to pay higher prices for imports. If their demand for the product concerned is inelastic, many will continue to buy the import. Higher prices reduce their purchasing power and their demand for other products.

Retaliation

● When country A uses tariffs to cut imports, sales fall in the exporting country, B. Businesses there will reduce output, making some employees redundant. Incomes in country B will fall; businesses and individuals will have less money to spend on imports. Even if country B does not retaliate, it will cut back on buying Country A's exports because it has less money to spend on them.

● Tariffs reduce competition. Inevitably, businesses that are protected have little incentive to produce efficiently. With tariffs in place they can relax a bit. Over time, they may lose the capacity to strive for efficiency, cut costs and sell at keen prices. Ultimately their customers will be the losers.

In the Great Depression, in the 1930s, protectionism made matters much worse than they need have been.

Beggar-thy-neighbour policies

Trade protection can have very serious consequences and can turn a recession into a depression. In the Great Depression, in the 1930s, protectionism made matters much worse than they need have been. Protectionist measures became known as beggar-thy-neighbour policies. Nowadays import controls can have very complex issues because of global supply chains. Domestically produced goods may have imported components. Tariffs on these would raise prices, making the domestic producer less competitive both in the home market and in export markets. Such unintended consequences would be hard to avoid.

Quotas

Quotas set a physical limit on imports of individual products. If demand is at a low level anyway, they will make no difference. But if demand is high, as in Figure 2, the price will be pushed up. Consumers will pay a higher price for a smaller quantity than they would ideally like to buy.

Figure 2: The effect of a quota

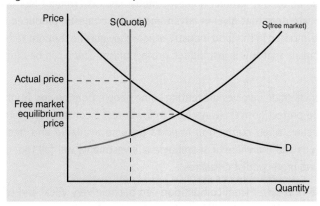

Substitutes

Exporters who are faced with quotas may in fact make increased profits from the higher prices they can charge when quantity is restricted. This will happen if there are few domestically produced competing products, i.e. good substitutes. The more price inelastic demand is, the more the price is likely to rise when a quota is imposed. Quotas almost always inhibit competition, leading to inefficiency.

Clothing prices

Using quotas

The most famous example of quotas was the Multi Fibre Arrangement (MFA), which ran from 1974 until 2004. It limited the amounts of clothing that many developing countries could export to the developed countries. It was designed to give the developed countries time to adjust to rising imports resulting from growing industrialisation in Asia. After 30 years, the WTO and many politicians thought that textile and clothing manufacturers in the developed countries had had time to adjust.

So in 2005. clothing prices dropped. Consumers were delighted to be able to buy cheap, fun clothing. Almost all the retailers were happy; H&M, Matalan and Primark had a field day. The proportion of total incomes spent on clothing fell, so other businesses benefited too as consumers could afford to buy more of other things.

In its 2015-16 annual report, Burberry said: "We announced in November a £50m initial investment in a new trench coat weaving and manufacturing facility, to be located in Leeds, Yorkshire. The new facility will bring increased capacity and greater efficiency, securing the future production of the trench and offering scope to develop and produce other products in the future."

1. Identify all the groups that gained from ending the MFA.

2. Explain which types of business would have lost out when the MFA quotas went and explain why.

3. Burberry was set up in 1856. Explain possible reasons for the company's survival and its optimism in 2016.

Other trade barriers

There are other kinds of protectionist policies, besides tariffs and quotas.

Subsidies

- Using subsidies to help a domestic industry can help it to compete. They may finance investment that raises productivity and cuts costs. Or they may simply allow the business to survive recession and continue in easier times. Government grants to US car producers in 2008-9 staved off imminent collapse but carried a requirement to restructure completely and close down uneconomic car plants. Both the US and the EU have subsidised Boeing and Airbus respectively, and both have complained about each other to the WTO.

- Keeping the exchange rate undervalued is a form of protection. The US government has sometimes accused China of manipulating its exchange rate to keep it low and strengthen Chinese exporters' competitiveness. The extent of Chinese exchange rate manipulation is disputed.

Safety standards

- Safety standards can be used to protect domestic industries. Government legislation can be framed in such a way as to create rules that give an advantage to the domestic producer. Nowadays these rules are most likely to be imposed in the food industry, where they may be thought to be necessary. However, some exporters complain that this is just hidden protectionism. There can be a fine line between safety and protection.

Any measure that restricts trade involves preventing some people from buying from the cheapest or best-value supplier. So trade protection will always lead to lower real incomes in the long run. The problem is that industries do decline when competing imports become available and decline is painful. Some employees lose their jobs and the value of shareholders' investments will fall too. Both groups will lobby the government, seeking protectionist measures.

Businesses and people who suffer from competition can become very vocal and sometimes get popular support for their efforts to get protection. The trouble is, protectionist measures always in the end make all consumers worse off and consumers as a whole are not an organised group. Protection may also deprive many businesses of chances to export successfully because of retaliation.

WTO

The work of the WTO and its international trade agreements have kept the use of tariffs and quotas at quite a low level for many years, at least in the manufacturing sector. The future however is rather unclear. There could be further negotiations to reduce trade barriers in the field of agriculture and services. Or populist political forces could push for more import controls. Meantime the WTO uses its dispute resolution mechanism to deal with individual member countries' disagreements.

Exam style question (Paper 1)

Evidence A – A global glut of steel

China produces about half the world's steel. But there are strong competitors in the EU, US, India, Korea and Japan. In 2014-15, it was obvious that investment in China was slowing down. Much investment involves steel and the consequence was a fall in steel sales – and prices.

The Chinese were accused of dumping. Tata Steel, the UK's biggest steel company, closed down part of its Llanwern mill in South Wales in 2015. All over the world steel mills were making employees redundant and reducing production. The EU imposed duties on certain types of steel, but stuck to the WTO rules.

Chinese officials threatened to retaliate and said "China safeguards the right to defend Chinese businesses in accordance with the rules of the WTO." They said they would look at ways to close down underutilised capacity.

Evidence B – Higher tariffs?

In 2016, the EU put tariffs on unfairly traded steel. However, EU tariffs were far lower than US tariffs imposed for the same reason. The EU tariff on dumped Chinese cold rolled steel was 16%; the US tariff for the same product was 266%.

Charles de Lusignan of Eurofer (EU steel producers organisation) said: *"European steel and UK steel is viable, so there is no fundamental reason why it shouldn't go on for the foreseeable future. The UK and others continue to block a proposal which would lead to higher tariffs, which means that when the government says it's doing everything it can to save the steel industry in the UK and also in Europe, it's not."*

Questions

1. Explain why dumping is seen as unfair. *(4 marks)*

2. Calculate the price difference between the USA and the EU when tariffs are applied to a Chinese steel product with a world price of $1,000. (Answer on page 107.) *(4 marks)*

3. Assess the effect of slowing investment in China on steel prices. *(10 marks)*

4. Assess the likelihood that "European steel and UK steel is viable." *(12 marks)*

5. Evaluate the effects that increased import controls could have (a) in the short run and (b) in the long run, on businesses, individuals and economies. *(20 marks)*

Chapter 5

Trading blocs

Free trade
areas

NAFTA

The North American Free Trade Area is a trading bloc that allows more or less free trade between Canada, the USA and Mexico. Since it was set up in 1994, the three member countries have become much more economically integrated. USA businesses gradually outsourced many production processes to Mexico, where imported components are assembled to become finished products for export. Many jobs have been created. Canada and the USA gained new, large and accessible markets on their doorsteps. Most analysts think that many people in Mexico have benefited from NAFTA. Jobs have been created in the car industry and Mexican farmers have been able to sell more of their products in the US. Consumers in the US have benefited from lower prices. However, Donald Trump thinks that NAFTA does not help the USA. If he became President of the US he would try to reduce trade with Mexico.

Discussion points

Work out what would happen to businesses in Canada, Mexico and the US if trade between them is substantially reduced.

Trading blocs are becoming increasingly important in the global economy. They are groups of regions or states that join together to reduce or eliminate trade barriers between each other. They encourage specialisation and open up new markets. The businesses that are the most competitive can grow faster and cut costs by reaping economies of scale. This gives businesses a chance to make more profit while consumers achieve greater purchasing power and higher standards of living.

Trading blocs fall broadly into several groups. There are **free trade areas**, like NAFTA. The Association of South East Asian Nations, ASEAN, is striving to become a **common market**. The EU is a **single market**.

Common
markets

Free trade areas are groups of countries that trade completely freely with each other, with no trade barriers, but each member country retains its own independent trade policies in relation to the rest of the world.

Common markets have completely free trade internally and a single unified trade policy covering all member countries' trade with the rest of the world (i.e. a common external tariff system). But besides free movement of goods and services, there is also free movement of people and capital. Individuals in all member countries can work in any other member country. Businesses based within a common market can invest in any member country.

Single markets go one stage beyond a common market. They remove all barriers to the movement of goods, labour and capital between member countries. They also aim to facilitate trade in services. A single market is close to being like a single economy. Regulations are harmonised so that product standards and working conditions are similar for all.

The European Union and the single market

The single
market

The EU started out as a common market; over the years it has progressed, getting closer and closer to becoming a single market. As of 2016, it has 500 million consumers and there is no doubt at all that it has increased trade between its members. The overall objective of the EU was always to achieve faster economic growth. Many people looked to achieve political integration as well as economic integration, but for many reasons this has not happened.

The move towards the single market began in the late 1980s, greatly encouraged by Prime Minister Thatcher. It was supposed to be complete by 1992. In fact it turned out to be an ongoing process. The idea was to create a level playing field, so that competing businesses would face similar requirements wherever production is located, and wherever they were selling their products, within the EU.

Harmonisation

Example

In a single market, safety requirements for products are the same for all. Businesses can create a standardised product and sell it right across the EU, rather than having to make slightly different products to suit each national market. This harmonisation makes possible long production runs and economies of scale.

Another objective of the single market is to enable people to work, and businesses to invest, in any member country, wherever would be most profitable. Free movement of people involves ensuring that professional qualifications gained in one country are recognised in all other member countries. Free movement of capital requires that governments allow FDI flows both into and out of their economies.

Think!

Within the EU, car seats for babies must all conform to common safety requirements. How does this make life easier for manufacturers of baby car seats in the EU? Identify one other product that is covered by EU regulations. (It is not true that bent bananas and curved cucumbers cannot be sold in the EU.)

EU history

Expansion

The EU has moved through various incarnations. It started life as the European Economic Community in 1957, with six member countries, Belgium, France, Germany, Italy, Luxembourg and the Netherlands. The UK joined in 1973, along with several other countries. In 2004 and after, many eastern European countries joined. The ex-Yugoslav countries are moving towards membership (Croatia has already joined); Turkey still hopes to develop a closer relationship with the EU. Norway and Iceland have looser links with the EU as part of the European Economic Area (EEA).

Trading relationships

BREXIT

In the June of 2016 the UK voted by a narrow majority to leave the EU. The specifications for your course were agreed before it became clear that the referendum would be held. Despite the result, you need to know about the EU, how it works and how closely the UK economy is still linked to it.

It took many years for the UK to settle into the EU. Getting out may take longer. Negotiating new trading relationships will be very difficult; the supporters of Brexit are very far from agreeing how they want to achieve their objective at the time of writing. It is quite probable that many of them have little knowledge or understanding of how exit might be achieved without excessive disruption. Many unintended consequences may emerge with time.

It is certain that to start with, there will be a long period in which little changes. Make sure you understand the current situation at the time when you are reading this.

The impact of the EU

New markets

Many new opportunities have been created by the development of the EU. Enlargement to 28 countries made it possible for eastern European countries to grow faster. But it also opened up new markets for the original 15 members, including the UK. For businesses, it provided a choice of locations where lower cost labour was readily available within the union.

The European Commission is the administrative heart of the EU. It is accountable to the European Parliament and has the power to initiate policy proposals so it is highly influential. But the individual member countries meet regularly through the Council of Ministers and can easily make themselves heard both individually and collectively.

Harmonisation in the single market

Harmonisation means ensuring that all regulatory controls on businesses are common to all EU member countries. It creates a level playing field for businesses. For example:

Competition law

● Labour laws require employers to avoid endangering or exploiting their employees; this can raise production costs. But if all the competing businesses within the EU have to stick to the same rules, none of them are disadvantaged when competing with each other.

● All businesses in the EU have to abide by EU competition law, as well as the laws of their own country. This prevents unfair competition by outlawing market-sharing agreements that could allow certain businesses to get away with charging higher prices than they would if they were competing. This has had a significant effect on competition and has led to consumers being charged lower prices for better quality products. It may be one of the most important benefits of EU membership for consumers.

● The single market involved the end of border controls on traded goods. This greatly reduced the amount of paperwork and the delays that used to occur at border crossings. There is no doubt that the single market approach has contributed to the integration of EU economies.

Tax incentives and welfare

However, tax and benefit systems are not harmonised. It would be impossible to secure agreement within the EU on this, at least for now. So there are still very real differences between member countries as to tax rates and benefit levels. France and Germany pay higher unemployment benefits than the UK. This may mean that incentives to work are less strong in those countries and may in part explain their higher unemployment rates in recent years. The UK's tax credit system does (for now) give many people a strong incentive to find work.

ASEAN

The Association of South East Asian Nations was initially set up in 1967 by Indonesia, Malaysia, Philippines, Singapore and Thailand, with the objective of becoming a free trade area, and operating in a very collaborative way. Great emphasis was placed on *cooperation in economic, social, cultural, technical, educational and other fields, and on the promotion of regional peace and stability.* The organisation is based in Jakarta, Indonesia.

Trade in Asia

In 2010, an agreement between ASEAN and China came into being, creating a fully fledged trade bloc, the China-Asean Free Trade Area. Tariffs were eliminated on 70% of products. The total population of this group is 1.9 billion. Initially, the tariff reductions applied only to China and the six founder (core) members of ASEAN. For the remaining four ASEAN members, Burma, Laos, Cambodia and Vietnam, the target date was 2015.

Core ASEAN members have a collective population of 633 million people. Economic growth within the area averages a healthy 5%. The governments concerned hope that their collective GDP will rise by $48 billion by 2020, over and above the growth that might have been expected under the old trading arrangements. China expects to benefit from cheaper commodity imports. Businesses in Indonesia, Thailand and the Philippines are nervous – they may suffer from fiercer competition with Chinese manufactures. But they may find new markets in China. ASEAN also has bilateral regional trade agreements with Japan, South Korea, India, Australia and New Zealand.

ASEAN has a distinctive philosophy of relying on consensus to achieve agreement. However, the ASEAN secretariat is not large or well-funded so there are limits to how much progress can be achieved. China's ambitions to exert power in the South China Sea, which are not popular with neighbouring states, threaten political stability. That said, ASEAN does appear to offer considerable hope for co-operation, economic stability and peace.

NAFTA

The North American Free Trade Area is a good example of a free trade area. Some Americans have their doubts about it but it has opened up new markets for many businesses. Consumers in Canada and the US have had the benefit of highly competitive imports from Mexico. NAFTA has created jobs in all three countries. There is no common tariff structure; each member has its own policies on imports from economies outside NAFTA (see page 28.)

The impact on businesses of trading blocs

Larger markets

The reduction of barriers between member countries within trade blocs can have both positive and negative impacts on businesses. Gaining access to large markets means that many businesses have the potential to increases sales and profits. Without tariffs, exports fall in price and become more competitive. Businesses that rely on imports of raw materials and components from fellow member states will also see a reduction in price as tariffs are removed; this translates into a fall in costs and can give a competitive advantage.

A new example – the TPP
Vietnam is about to join 11 other countries, the US, Japan, Malaysia, Singapore, Brunei, Australia, New Zealand, Canada, Mexico, Chile and Peru in the Trans-Pacific Partnership agreement (TPP). The TPP aims to deepen economic ties between these nations and increase free trade and growth by reducing and abolishing around 18,000 tariffs. Sources estimate that Vietnam's GDP could grow by an extra $36bn over the next ten years if the deal goes ahead. Exports are expected to increase by 28% as it gains access to the lucrative markets of developed countries such as the USA, Japan and Australia. The clothing and footwear sector is expected to increase exports by 50%.

Vietnam is about to join 11 other countries in the Trans-Pacific Partnership agreement.

For consumers, imports become cheaper which increases their real income. Businesses that can export more will grow, creating employment and income. All of which means increased demand for goods and services. So businesses that have little connection with international trade such as shops, cinemas and restaurants can also benefit from the growth of trade.

There is, inevitably, a downside; reducing trade barriers also gives other member countries a chance to sell their goods and services without tariffs. Domestic businesses may face increased competition and if they do not have a competitive advantage, they may struggle. Businesses that previously exported to a country that has now joined a trade bloc may find their sales declining as they must now pay the tariffs imposed by the whole trade bloc. Some exporting businesses may close and unemployment may rise.

Trade creation and trade diversion

One of the features of a trade bloc is that it changes the patterns of trade. In time, more trade will take place within the bloc; trade increases between the member countries. This is called trade creation. Trade with countries outside of the bloc decreases, this is called trade diversion.

For many years after joining the EU, UK trade with EU member countries increased, relative to trade with the rest of the world. Recently, UK trade with the EU has shrunk from 52% to 48% of total foreign trade. This is most probably because of slow growth in the Eurozone economies, leading to falling demand.

The impact of the EU on firms in member countries includes:

● Access to larger markets, leading to rising exports.

● Increased competition which creates pressure to increase efficiency.

Efficiency

● Incentives to innovate and adapt to changing conditions.

● A single market, with abolition of border controls on the movement of goods, can reduce the costs of exporting and importing.

● Firms that cannot adapt or increase efficiency may close down or be taken over.

The European Competition Commission has been effective in pursuing firms that have engaged in anti-competitive practices. These include market sharing agreements and price fixing.

Anti-competitive practices

Example
In late 2009, the office of the EU Competition Commissioner investigated the market for car repairs. It found that car manufacturers had tried to protect their own dealers and repairers from competition in a number of ways, including withholding vital technical information from independent car repairers. Measures are being implemented to prevent this kind of protection and increase competition. Tackling anti-competitive practices has led to price cuts and improved efficiency in many businesses, contributing to economic growth.

Interdependence

Specialisation is all about buying the best-value product from wherever it is available. So buyers are often dependent on sourcing their requirements from other countries. But global interdependence is about capital, as well as consumer goods. Foreign direct investment (FDI), investing capital in other countries, has been highly significant in the development of new, competitive production facilities. The MNCs that are active in a number of economies have facilitated the growth of trade. Most of them see growth in their own turnover as an end in itself and a source of ever increasing profits.

International co-operation

A natural consequence of interdependence is that change in one economy will affect many other economies. The government policies of trading nations will have an impact far beyond their own borders. So there is a great need for international co-operation. However imperfect the international organisations are (and they usually are even more imperfect than national governments), we need them to facilitate collaboration and international agreement.

The G7 and G20 have proved important in providing opportunities for collaborative thinking, particularly when trading conditions become difficult, as in the financial crisis of 2008-9 and the slowdown in trade in

2015-16. International co-operation (fostered by WTO trade negotiations and agreements) helps to create global economic stability. This helps businesses to plan ahead and to develop bold investment projects.

There is much disquiet in developed economies about the extent to which jobs have been lost and wages reduced through trade liberalisation. This may change the pattern of international trade. If this happens, people and governments will be choosing to buy what they want at higher prices, so as to protect jobs. This may not help poor people who have not lost their jobs. Nor will it help businesses that have built up big export markets.

Exam style question – RCEP (Paper 1)

The Regional Comprehensive Economic Partnership (RCEP) is a proposed Free Trade Agreement (FTA) involving the 10 Association of Southeast Asian Nations (ASEAN) member states and its FTA partners Australia, China, India, Japan, Korea and New Zealand. The RCEP will include more than 3 billion people, with a combined GDP of $17 trillion, and account for 40% of world trade.

Among the countries involved, India is planning to reduce import tariffs further in the coming years, a proposal that may not get too much support from its domestic industries. In return, the Government is hoping to get a better deal for Indian nurses, teachers and auditors who want to work in any of the 16 initial members of the proposed RCEP, including Australia and New Zealand.

1. Explain two possible reasons why India might have placed tariffs on imports in the past. *(4 marks)*

2. Explain two ways in which the creation of the RCEP might affect UK businesses. *(4 marks)*

3. Assess the likely impact of increased movement of labour on the countries within the RCEP. *(10 marks)*

4. Assess the likely effects that the formation of RCEP might have on India's domestic industries. *(12 marks)*

5. Evaluate the extent to which free trade might improve standards of living, supporting your arguments with examples. *(20 marks)*

Chapter 6

Conditions that prompt trade

Terms to revise: market power, competitive markets, product and process innovation (Theme 1), economies of scale, diversifying, human capital, product life cycle extension strategies.

Primark

Associated British Foods is a major food processor and the second largest sugar producer in the world. It has a significant share of the bread market in the UK; in fact it is likely that you have eaten at least one of its products very recently indeed. Besides British Sugar, it owns Twinings Tea, Patak's (the Indian food business) and a host of other brands such as Ovaltine, Jordan's cereals and Ryvita.

Primark, the Irish clothing retailer, is a subsidiary of ABF. This massive network of companies has strong interests in international trade. Primark arrived in the UK in 1973 but its big expansion took place in the early 2000s. From 2006 it spread out across Europe. Sales rose by 150% between 2009 and 2014. In 2015 it opened its first shop in Boston, USA. More will follow and the USA is the world's biggest clothing market.

Primark reckons the demand for clothing is very price elastic; its USP is ultra-low prices that undercut the competition. These are possible because of:

● wafer-thin profit margins

● very carefully organised logistics so transport costs are minimised

● little spending on marketing

● bulk buying from suppliers to drive down costs

USA customers may love it. Primark's market growth may go up and up. But what are the risks?

● Primark doesn't do on-line selling. The prices are too low to make it worthwhile.

● Environmentalists don't approve of throwing away clothing.

● Some of the workers in the Rana Plaza factory building in Bangladesh, when it collapsed in 2013, were making clothes for Primark. The company paid $14 million to the victim's families.

These factors could make selling in the US difficult and unprofitable. But Primark's sales grew by 20% in 2014. It had 0.8% of the global market for clothing. Compare that with H&M, which had 1.8%. Primark's prices in 2015 were 22% lower than the nearest US competitor.

Discussion points

Why would Primark choose to expand internationally?

How successful might they be?

What's wrong with throwing away clothing?

There are many reasons why a business may seek out a new overseas market. Some can be described as either 'Push' or 'Pull' factors.

> A **Push factor** is something that happens within an existing market that forces a business to look elsewhere for survival or success.
>
> A **Pull factor** is something that happens in another market that attracts a business towards it, so that it can take advantage of the conditions.

Push factors: saturated markets and competition

It would be hard for Primark to expand its market share in the UK and Ireland. They could open more outlets but most people can already reach one fairly easily. Growth would be modest and any increase in market share would be small. Primark is getting close to **market saturation** in its home territories.

> **Market saturation** occurs when it becomes impossible to expand sales further in that particular market. If the product is a durable good, e.g. a washing machine, it may still be possible to sell replacement machines. But growth will be difficult.

It is no accident that Primark expanded when it did. In 2004 there was a global agreement to cut tariffs on clothing (see page 26). Low wage economies immediately increased their output of cheap clothing. Primark worked out ways of cutting costs and prices and so acquired a competitive advantage in distribution.

Diversifying

Market saturation is a major factor in international trade. Successful businesses are constantly looking for ways to reach a larger market. Some diversify their product range to attract more domestic customers but often, exporting existing products will be easiest. Much depends on the level of competition in potential foreign markets. Primark looks safe on price, at least in the US and Europe. But supposing the US customers don't warm to their styles and quality? Using Ansoff's matrix could help to plan appropriate strategies in this situation.

> **Find out**
> Look for information on Primark sales in the USA. Company reports may comment.

Looking for new markets

Adapting to change

Some businesses look to emerging markets for expansion. Rising incomes in emerging economies can make for excellent opportunities. When Vodafone found its UK and EU market shares declining, it branched out into India and Turkey. This was difficult at first and Vodafone had to adapt their offer to suit economies where most people lived on very modest incomes. But in 2015 its sales in Europe dropped by 8%, while sales in emerging markets rose by 6%. Emerging markets offer good opportunities for expansion; competition is often less of a problem than it is in developed economies.

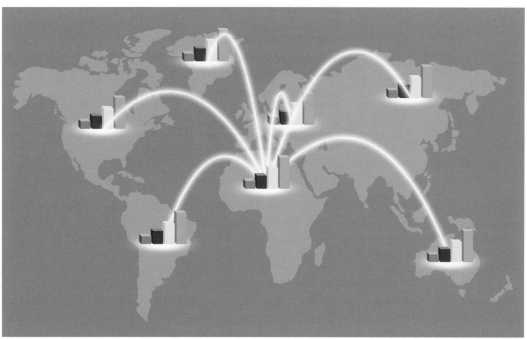

Emerging markets offer good opportunities for expansion.

Example

Vodafone in Africa

In many parts of Africa, laying land-lines was far too costly to be considered. It was much cheaper to put up mobile masts. Many people survive on low incomes but one of the first things they get when incomes improve is a mobile. Vodafone came up with a mobile money transfer system for Kenya, known as M-PESA. This helped ordinary people to set up small businesses. It has been very successful and now operates in South Africa, Afghanistan, India and Eastern Europe as well. Of course, the resulting growth in incomes has benefited Vodafone too.

The CMA

The mobile market is exceptionally dynamic. But on a more modest level, similar conditions apply to many businesses. Competition from other producers can create a tough trading environment. Governments in developed countries want to encourage competition. In the UK, the Competition and Markets Authority (CMA) works to prevent individual businesses from acquiring too much market power. Competition policy keeps prices down for consumers and it gives businesses an incentive to produce efficiently. Businesses in competitive markets often find that they cannot easily expand their market share in their domestic market. So they seek out overseas markets.

Pull factors: economies of scale and risk factors

Achieving economies of scale

Where there is healthy competition, market share in the domestic economy may be insufficient to allow the business to reach its optimum size. That means that output for the domestic market is not high enough to reap all potential economies of scale.

Jaguar Land Rover (JLR)

Under its Indian parent company, Tata Motors, JLR has grown dramatically. This is based partly on cost cutting. Between 2010 and 2015, sales and employment doubled and sales revenue tripled. It is not a big company, as car manufacturers go, but it sells 500,000 vehicles per year into its global market. This is sufficient to create the economies of scale that make the company viable.

Figure 1: JLR sales by region

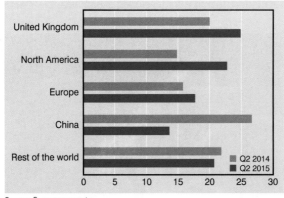

Source: Company reports

Product and process innovation

Economies of scale are often related to innovations which may, initially, be quite costly to develop. These could be new product developments or improvements in the design of existing products. (Both of these are product innovations.) Or they could be process innovations that cut costs by finding better production strategies.

A business with a small domestic market may provide insufficient sales revenue to make expensive innovations worth the cost of research and development (R&D). The prospect of sales in foreign markets greatly increases the expected future income stream from any proposed innovation and may reduce risks.

Example – Airbus

In the aircraft industry, development costs can overrun. Airbus competes vigorously with Boeing. How could Airbus possibly have risked developing the A380, its newest wide-bodied airliner, if it did not have a global market? There were interminable glitches in the development process – there usually are, with new aircraft. These pushed up the cost. But the advance orders from several different airlines provided the incentive to carry on.

Innovation

Some products are constantly being superseded by technical change and innovation. This always happens with machines and electrical goods – cars, computers, smartphones and so on. Suppliers have to keep abreast of new technologies, patent their own discoveries and innovate as fast as they can, just to stay in business. An international market increases the incentives to keep on researching potential innovations and reduces the risks. Sales may drop off in one market but are less likely to diminish in all markets at once. Competing companies will be innovating too, and maintaining competitiveness means keeping up and if possible surpassing the achievements of rival businesses.

Think!

JLR's sales in China fell in 2015 because of a crackdown on corruption. Fewer people had incomes large enough to buy JLR vehicles. How might JLR react to this?

Minimising risk

Some businesses just become addicted to expansion. If their home market is saturated, they may go on a shopping spree, looking for inorganic growth and buying up appropriate businesses abroad. Or they may set up their own factories or offices or retail outlets, growing organically wherever they feel confident of being able to create a new market. This process explains much of current FDI. Diversifying into different markets reduces the risks associated with expansion. Falling sales in one market may be offset by rising sales in another.

Global sourcing – offshoring

For many businesses, expansion overseas opens up new markets. For others the primary objective may be to find new locations for production, where costs will be lower. They seek out locations with the lowest wage costs but also with the necessary skills. This is offshoring.

When thinking about global sourcing it is helpful to look at the production process as a supply chain. This starts with the purchasing of the inputs, follows through the process of creating the product, moving the product to the point of sale and finalising the payment process. Inputs will come from a wide range of sources. For each input there will be alternatives.

Diverse supply chains

Example

Intel manufactures most of its high technology products (the processors) in the USA. But these are just the components – most of the assembly processes are carried out in Asia. Korea had a long term advantage in this field, starting out with cheap labour working for Intel in the 1980s. Then as Korea prospered, wages rose and Intel moved its assembly stage to south east Asia (mainly China, Malaysia and Vietnam) where wages were lower.

Now, Intel locates some sales, marketing and R&D activities in Korea, which has the appropriately skilled labour that they need for this work. Similarly Dyson is doing well producing in Malaysia, where wages are far from being the lowest but scarce skills are available.

Examples

Nike and Primark subcontract all of their production to independent businesses located in economies with low wage rates.

Apple entrusts much of its production process to Foxconn, the giant Taiwanese electronics business located in Shenzhen, China.

JLR is offshoring some work to an Austrian business, while looking for a future production site in eastern Europe.

There is nothing to stop businesses from continuing to base their production in their home location, while offshoring just one or more processes in the supply chain.

Offshoring specific parts of the supply chain

Example

One UK manufacturer of high quality men's shoes wanted to continue producing in the UK but was fighting rising wage costs that could not be passed on by raising prices. So they looked at the most labour intensive part of the production process – stitching the leather uppers. They subcontracted this to a Thai factory which had access to cheaper but skilled labour. They were still able to control the quality of the product and claim with some justice that it was made in the UK. The cost savings were well above the extra transport costs. Their supply chain looked like this:

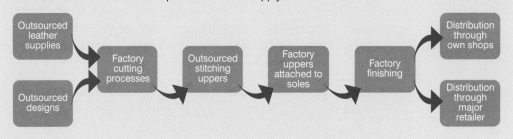

Offshoring can yield substantial cost savings, enhancing competitive advantage, especially if the product can be standardised for a range of markets. Unskilled labour may be cheaper, more available and less regulated. Many countries now offer labour that is cheap, skilled and adaptable as well.

Specialist consulting firms will help businesses to find appropriate offshoring opportunities. Hong Kong consultants have detailed knowledge of Chinese businesses and can supply foreign companies with valuable information. Advice can help to reduce the risks associated with offshoring and sub-contracting.

Find out

Look at Li and Fung's website. Scroll down and select The Fung Group. It offers business to business services (B2B). What kind of business might find this useful?

Reshoring

Offshoring is not a permanent solution. Costs change over time and it may be that the business needs to relocate its production if this happens. Labour costs in China are rising and in some areas a minimum wage has been introduced. Although labour costs remain low the difference may no longer be enough to compensate for the delivery costs and time taken for shipping. As a result, some businesses that have outsourced their production to China are moving to another country with cheaper labour (e.g. Vietnam). Others are bringing production back home in a process known as **onshoring** or **reshoring**.

Outsourcing

Some production is entirely offshored. Other products are created and marketed entirely within one economy – this is common in the service sector. Many supply chains involve outsourcing. This means that they buy a range of inputs from supplier businesses and locations, which may or may not involve offshoring.

> **Outsourcing** is a general term for buying inputs from independent suppliers, either within the same economy or abroad. It can apply to any inputs, components, or finished products, or business services such as cleaning, accountancy or IT services.

Much offshoring may be referred to as outsourcing. But the business that invests in building its own factories or distribution centres within foreign economies is offshoring but not outsourcing, because it has complete control of its own facilities. Think of JCB with its own factories in India.

Many businesses outsource by buying inputs from suppliers locally or within their own economy. Other businesses provide inputs or services to customer businesses that are outsourcing some part of their supply chain (B2B). Think of JLR buying vehicle components from other businesses in the West Midlands.

Businesses have many options about how they organise their supply chains and take their location decisions.

Businesses have many options about how they organise their supply chains and take their location decisions. They need to be nimble and adaptable. They must make careful cost comparisons and be very much aware of the trade-off between low-cost labour and quality human capital. Above all they need to be responsive to change in the markets where they buy and sell. These include labour markets and commodity markets where they buy raw materials. Good access to information is really critical. Both moving into new markets and relocating production often make sense, but only if carried out with great care and detailed feasibility studies that identify possible risks.

Location decisions may involve markets or raw material sources

Producing close to markets

Cheap production locations are not the only consideration. Many businesses want to locate production close to their markets. Japanese car companies in the UK want to be inside the EU; Toyota, the world's biggest car manufacturer, has expanded significantly in the USA, considerably reducing the market share of the US motor industry.

Raw materials

Other businesses may locate facilities close to their raw material sources. This may or may not involve outsourcing but it is likely to create at least some jobs for local people. Examples include minerals, petrochemicals and many commodity industries. MNCs are exploiting Arctic mineral and oil reserves. They may try to secure resources for future growth by preventing rivals from acquiring them.

> **Example**
> Bolivia sits on 50-70 % of the world's lithium reserves. Lithium batteries are commonly used today to operate computers, smartphones, and other portable electronic devices. Demand may increase dramatically if electric cars are mass-produced and consume a growing share of the market. MNCs such as Toyota are keen to gain access to these reserves but the Bolivian government wants to make the most of this potentially valuable resource.

Extending product life cycles

What can a business do when its product has passed through the growth and maturity phases of the product life cycle and is going into decline? Extension strategies can work. Improvements and subtle changes in the product may help it to maintain sales. But new markets may provide more sales growth than could be achieved in the domestic market through minor product changes. The big tobacco companies like BAT

(British American Tobacco) and Philip Morris International have successfully targeted emerging markets and also some very poor countries with massive advertising campaigns. But they are not the only ones.

Selling scotch whisky

In 2014, scotch exports fell by 7.4%. In 2015, Alexandre Ricard, chairman of Pernod Ricard, which owns Chivas Regal, came to Scotland to be present when First Minister Nicola Sturgeon opened a brand new distillery alongside the River Spey. He pointed out that his business had grown by 4% in 2014. Chivas had seen strong growth in demand for single malts in the US. Pernod Ricard's other brand, Glenlivet, is doubling capacity to 10m litres per year. The company sees big growth prospects in India, where the youthful population brings 22 million new drinking-age consumers into the market every year. There is talk of innovation too, of new flavours that can be introduced into blended whiskies.

Questions

1. Why might whisky producers be worrying about demand?

2. Why might they expect to succeed in new markets?

3. To what extent are they taking risks?

4. Identify two luxury or fashion producers that might survive shrinking domestic markets in a similar way, and explain your choice.

If tastes or fashions are involved, or if technologies have improved, the decline phase of the product life cycle may be surprisingly swift. But extension strategies are not impossible.

Example

Microsoft and Nokia

Adaptation for a new market

Early in 2015, Microsoft (which owns Nokia) unveiled a cheap, internet-enabled Nokia phone costing $29. It can run Facebook, Twitter and other apps. Features include a radio and a torch. It is robust and durable and has a battery said to last 29 days on standby. It is built for difficult terrains and functions where electricity is unreliable. It may not sell well in emerging or developed markets but it should make a big difference in any economy where there are still large numbers of poor people. It may turn out to be very profitable for Microsoft.

Signs of a slowdown

Slower growth in trade

Trade is not growing so fast as it was before the financial crisis, 2008-9. Figure 2 shows how for many years, trade grew faster than economic growth. Since the recovery, it has been stable. This is partly because China's growth rate has slowed. If India grows faster for a while, further trade expansion may follow. It will be important to watch the data carefully over the next few years.

Figure 2: Flows of goods, services and FDI as % of global GDP

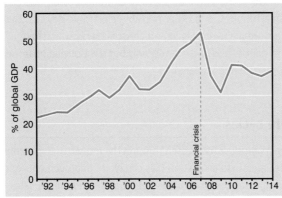

Source: IMF

Exam style question

Evidence

- General Electric in the USA is using 3D printers to make fuel nozzles for jet engines. It expects to be making extensive use of this technology by 2020.

- Global supply chains are shortening, partly due to reshoring but also because Chinese manufacturers are now producing the components that they used to import just for assembly.

- Car companies are both reshoring and concentrating their overseas plant in places where sales are promising.

- China is looking for more customers along its 'New Silk Road'.

- Robots are expected to be used for more assembly operations in the next few years.

Question

Using the above information and evidence from case studies in this chapter, evaluate the likely changes in international trade and their probable impact on businesses over the next decade.

(20 marks)

Terms to revise: exchange rates, appreciation and depreciation.

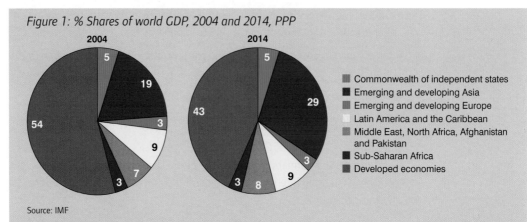

Figure 1: % Shares of world GDP, 2004 and 2014, PPP

Source: IMF

Figure 1 is complicated to interpret, but very revealing:

- The Commonwealth of Independent States includes Russia and the other ex-members of the USSR (Russia as it was before 1989).

- Sub-Saharan Africa had 3% of world GDP in 2004 and in 2014. This doesn't mean it hasn't had economic growth. It means that its growth rate has on average been the same as the global rate of growth.

- The big change is in the balance between developed economies and emerging economies in Asia.

Discussion points
1. Does this mean that EU businesses should invest in successful Asian economies but not in, say, the USA?

2. What can it tell businesses about where to seek export marketing opportunities?

There are many different business situations in which globalised activities take place. Some can be grouped together because they all want to expand into new markets. These include:

Searching for markets

- Exporters looking for markets and using agents in the importing country to facilitate sales.

- Businesses investing in productive capacity or distribution facilities outside their own economy, in order to be close to and sell in overseas markets.

- Businesses providing finance for investment outside their own economy, in order to make a good rate of return.

In the course of planning, businesses in these situations will be examining the factors that influence expansion and how they can assess the attractiveness of different markets.

Level and growth of disposable income

Finding buyers

Exporters need to know what the possibilities are in a range of economies, so that they can size up the likely profitability of the market. A growing market suggests promise, but much depends on the way income is distributed and the current per capita income. High taxes may be a factor too; disposable income is income after tax. Table 1 on page 2 shows growth rates for the UK and a range of emerging and developing countries.

Table 1 below shows recent economic growth in developed economies, while Figure 2 shows where the buyers of luxury goods are to be found. Table 2 shows per capita incomes and days to set up a business for several emerging and developed economies.

Demand for luxuries

Table 1: Economic growth rates in the developed world

	2013	2014	2015
USA	1.5	2.4	2.4
Canada	2.2	2.5	1.1
France	0.6	0.3	1.2
Germany	0.3	1.6	1.7
Japan	1.4	0.0	0.5

Source World Bank

Figure 2: Global luxury goods market, 2015, %

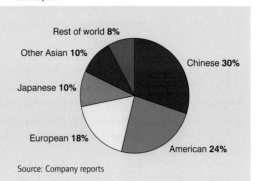

Source: Company reports

Table 2: Per capita income, US$ at PPP and days to start a business

Country	Per capita income	Days to set up a business	Country	Per capita income	Days to set up a business
China	14,239	31	USA	55,837	6
India	6,020	29	UK	41,325	5
Brazil	15,359	83	Germany	47,268	11
S. Africa	13,165	46	Japan	37,322	10
Russia	24,451	11	Korea	34,549	4

Source: World Bank, 2015

Example

China

Growth has been strong for many years, taxes are low and some people have become extremely wealthy. They have provided a good market for exporters of luxury goods (Louis Vuitton, Burberry, expensive wines from France, JLR cars etc.). In 2013 luxury goods sales growth was 33%. However, after 2010 the economic growth rate slowed and in 2015, President Xi Jinping led an anti-corruption drive. People are spending less on luxuries. The future is uncertain.

Middle-income markets

Very low incomes suggest limited demand for imports. But many businesses will be seeking to target consumers in the 'growing middle class'. These people are not the wealthy earners who will buy luxury goods but those who have benefited from the development of the economy. Possibly for the first time, they have surplus disposable income and are looking to improve their lifestyle by buying consumer goods such as microwaves, televisions, fridges and washing machines. The leisure market will also be expanding now that consumers have time and money for recreation, so the demand for tourism, sports kit, films and the arts should lead to expansion.

Example

In China, Disney has just opened its biggest ever theme park in Shanghai. Thomas Cook has just entered into a joint venture with a Chinese partner, Fosun International. This is to take advantage of the growing tourism market as more Chinese take a holiday both within China and overseas.

Show your understanding

Using the data above, decide where you might try to sell (a) scotch whisky and (b) IT products. Explain your reasoning.

It is very easy to google both per capita income and days to start a business if you are trying to find out about economies not already mentioned. Add 'World Bank' to your search.

Regulation

Ease of doing business

Any business planning to sell or invest abroad will want to know about all aspects of doing business. Many countries have complex regulations that make it quite difficult for anyone to set up a business, let alone foreigners.

The World Bank publishes an annual report called *Doing Business*, which measures regulations affecting 11 areas of the life of a business. These include starting a business, dealing with construction permits, getting electricity, registering property, getting credit, paying taxes, trading across borders, enforcing contracts and resolving insolvency. The result is a ranking of the 189 countries from the easiest to do business in, to the most difficult.

Table 3: Ease of doing business index, 2016

Rank		Rank	
1	Singapore	184	D.R. Congo
2	New Zealand	185	Chad
3	Hong Kong	186	South Sudan
4	Denmark	187	Central African Republic
5	South Korea	188	Libya
6	UK	189	Eritrea

Source: World Bank

Reforms

Although the last six countries shown in Table 3 are in Africa, it is worth noting that Sub-Saharan Africa, the region with the largest number of economies, accounted for the largest number of regulatory reforms in 2013/14. 39 countries were reducing the complexity and cost of regulatory processes and 36 strengthened their legal institutions.

> **Find out**
> Using the latest World Bank *Doing Business* report find out:
> - Current rankings.
> - Which countries have improved the most.
> - Where the BRICS and MINT countries are ranked.

On the whole, emerging economies tend to make setting up a business harder than developed economies do. With all foreign countries, there may be other issues – such as cultural differences and language barriers. (There is more on this in Chapter 13.) One thing is clear. If a business is looking to expand into new markets, it will need competent people who can negotiate deals and ensure that it does not fall foul of the law. People like this are easier to find in some countries than in others.

Legal systems

A second aspect of the ease of doing business concerns whether or not the legal system will provide protection in the event of things going wrong. In many emerging economies, the legal system is slow and rather unpredictable. The costs of mishaps may have to be carried. For example, if customers don't pay, court action may not help.

Infrastructure

It goes without saying that exporting businesses have to know how they are going to communicate with the agents who will be marketing and distributing their exports. Recruiting people who know and understand the local situation and have language skills will be important but they must have reliable access to internet and phone connections.

Infrastructure

Transport facilities have to be adequate for purpose too. Ports, airports, roads, railways and container ships must meet exporters' requirements. The World Bank has a Logistics Performance Index which is very accessible and scores all economies according to their transport facilities. This makes it very easy for businesses to decide which potential export markets they will be able to reach easily.

> **Example**
> For businesses such as Walmart, trying to break into African and Asian markets, infrastructure is very important. The problems of distributing foods and other perishable goods over sometimes inadequate road systems can be considerable.

Much depends upon the type of market that exporters are trying to reach. Access to distribution facilities for luxury goods will not usually be a problem because the customers will anyway be located in bigger cities. Setting up outlets will be relatively easy. A company like Unilever that aims to reach people on all income levels, will need a much wider range of distribution strategies. Unilever markets its products in 190 countries.

Political stability

Governments that resent the presence of foreign businesses in their economies occasionally talk about nationalising them – but rarely actually take them over. Mostly they are glad to have the injection of FDI and the resulting jobs for local people. Foreigners who bring in other foreigners to run their businesses are not so popular because there will be few if any benefits for the host country.

Avoiding war zones

The World Bank's per capita GDP data suggests that wars cause extreme poverty. There is no data for Syria for the past 4 years but South Sudan's Gross National Income per capita at PPP prices went from $2320 in 2011 to $1800 in 2014, as violence escalated. Compare this with the emerging markets in Table 1, page 2. Some war-torn economies have grown fast once the violence ended. It is no surprise to find that investors avoid signs of political instability.

There is more corruption in some economies than in others but on the whole, businesses seem to weather this problem most of the time. Corruption often hinders economic development but some countries, e.g. China, seem to grow anyway. Transparency International is a respected source of information on corruption.

Exchange rates

Exchange rates were covered very briefly in Theme 2. There is no doubt that exchange rate changes can have a big impact on business earnings and create potential risks.

Depreciation

● Businesses investing abroad will be disadvantaged by *depreciation* because the local currency they buy to pay for the facilities that they are building will cost them more in terms of their domestic currency. However, businesses that are exporting domestically produced goods and services will make substantial gains because the new exchange rate will make their products cheaper to buy in foreign currency. They will have a choice between reducing prices, or keeping them the same so that profits are higher. They may of course do both – cutting prices but by less than the rate of the depreciation.

Appreciation

● Similarly, businesses looking for new export markets will be disadvantaged by *appreciation* – their products will become less competitive. They will probably sell less or cut the price and make less profit, i.e. absorb some or all of the effects of appreciation. This may be less important for those companies that import some inputs that are used to create the final product that they plan to export.

Most businesses factor in potential exchange rate losses. Some investors are able to use forward markets where they can lock into a known exchange rate for the date when they need the currency but this may not be cheap. Importers can do the same when they are setting up purchase agreements. These strategies reduce risks. Here, again, careful consideration is needed before taking decisions.

Selling insurance in Cambodia

On the face of it Cambodia does not look like a great place to sell insurance. It is still very poor, even though its horrific war ended in 1979. The economy developed very slowly at first. Its infrastructure is still very limited and for ease of doing business, it is ranked 135. But Prudential Insurance must think there is hope.

On the riverside in Phnom Penh.

Exam style question (Paper 1)

Africa may become a significant market for global businesses over the next few decades.

- At the moment some 22 African countries with a combined population of 400 million have middle income status (over $1,000 per capita per year).

- By 2025 that is expected to have increased to 32 countries and 600 million people.

- At the moment Africa has more middle class households than India.

- Africa's population is 900 million (7% of global total), by 2050 it is predicted to be 1.96 billion (21% of global total).

- By 2030 Africa's top 18 cities will have a spending power of $1.3 trillion.

- The IMF estimates that the future growth rate for sub-Saharan Africa in 2017 and beyond will average 6.1% compared to the global average of 4%.

- Walmart, the world's biggest company is expanding its presence in Africa with joint ventures and takeovers.

- Walmart currently has 172 outlets in 11 African countries and is opening up in Kenya and Nigeria, which is now Africa's biggest economy.

Questions

1. Explain two pull factors that may cause a global business to enter an African market. *(4 marks)*

2. Explain two push factors that may cause a global business to enter an African market. *(4 marks)*

3. Assess the possible impact on local businesses of Walmart's entry into African markets. *(10 marks)*

4. Assess the importance for a retailer of the level of disposable income when considering entering a new market in Africa. *(12 marks)*

5. Assess the potential difficulties for a global business when entering a new market in Africa. *(20 marks)*

Chapter 8

Assessment of a country as a production location

Make in India

Prime Minister Modi has high hopes. In 2016 he relaunched Make in India, a campaign to turn his country into a manufacturing powerhouse. India's population in 2015 was 1.31 billion while China's, with a lower birth rate, was 1.37. India's manufacturing sector was around 21% of GDP. In China, over 40% of GDP came from manufacturing. It seems likely that India will be able to offer lower wage rates than China for some time to come. With that and an education system that generates highly skilled people, India should be able to attract plenty of FDI and many companies seeking offshore capacity. Already:

● Ericsson, the Swedish electronic company, is planning a second factory in Pune. To date, it has 22,000 employees in India.

● Emerson, a US-based producer of control systems for industry, plans to add four more factories to its existing 17.

● Foxconn, the Taiwanese company that supplies Apple's iPhones, is planning 12 new factories with a million employees.

Figure 1: FDI inflows to India ($bn)

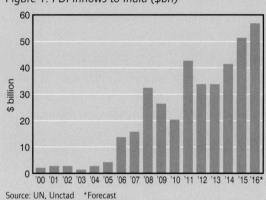

Source: UN, Unctad   *Forecast

Discussion point

What are the likely pros and cons of producing in India?

Factors influencing the location of production

Relocating production can be achieved by:

Relocating to cut costs

● Finding suppliers that will manufacture the product cheaply and to the standard required (outsourcing)

● Setting up new production facilities that are owned and operated by the company itself, albeit with the help of local managers, (offshoring).

Many of the issues relating to location planning and offshoring are the same as those relating to expanding markets. The ease of doing business, addressed on page 44, applies equally to considering production locations. Similarly, the requirement of political stability (page 45) is essentially the same for both.

Costs of production in foreign markets are a crucial factor in any location decision. Although many businesses are still finding that producing in China keeps costs down, others are finding that there is lower-cost labour elsewhere. They may move production to other Asian economies with lower wage rates, e.g. Vietnam, Indonesia and India. Or they may find that new manufacturing techniques are changing the cost balance between domestic and foreign production locations. This has led to some **reshoring**.

Reshoring

> **Reshoring** means producing close to the business HQ rather than offshoring or outsourcing. In 2012, General Electric decided to move its production of washing machines, fridges and heaters from China back to Kentucky.

As emerging economies grow, their wages rates are rising. So far it has been possible to move to different, cheaper emerging economies. The possibilities in India look promising and in time African economies may offer opportunities. However, more manufacturers may decide to produce close to their markets. In the meantime, examining costs of production is key to a successful decision about location. In particular, it will be necessary to consider the possibility of exchange rate changes because appreciation of the host country's currency will add to production costs.

> **Think!**
> When seeking low labour costs, many businesses can choose between outsourcing, i.e. buying from local suppliers, or offshoring, i.e. setting up their own factories in low cost locations. Nike outsources, while the examples in the case study above showed businesses investing in their own facilities. Explain how the businesses concerned might have made these decisions.

Skills and availability of labour force

Planning for a new location includes finding out how easy it will be to recruit labour with appropriate skills for the technologies that will be used. It may be that training programmes are necessary and must be budgeted for. (Sources for all inputs must be identified, including any natural resources that are needed.)

Productivity

What will labour costs be? There may be a trade off between paying low wages and recruiting people with the necessary human capital – the issue that led Dyson to Malaysia, where skilled people were readily available. Wage costs will be an important element in determining the likely rate of return from the venture. Skill levels affect productivity, which in turn affects costs per unit produced.

> **Example**
> Lingerie retailer Agent Provocateur manufacturers many of its more basic garments in China where labour costs are low. Its premium lines are made in Morocco where the wage costs are higher. However, the labour force has greater expertise to carry out the intricate and challenging work needed to maintain the quality the business relies on.

Infrastructure

Communication

Nimble businesses that function in dynamic markets and offshore all or part of their production need really good communications with their offshore suppliers. They need to be confident that orders will be delivered on time. Maintaining close communications will be important. Locations that have unreliable energy supplies or internet access will be at a disadvantage.

> **Example**
> The people who set up flower growing businesses in Kenya had to be sure that the flowers could be air-freighted out to European markets quickly. Local airports had to be capable of handling the business. Many developing economies have poor roads and port facilities, affecting choice of location. Investors sometimes have to negotiate with governments in order to get appropriate infrastructure built. They may also help to pay for it.

Energy

Easy communication will be very important for direct investors who have to acquire land, build and equip their plant, assemble a workforce and determine the organisation of production processes. Reliable energy and water supplies may be particularly important. Investors need considerable help from local people, meeting them and developing a good understanding. All this requires reliable communication facilities.

Businesses like Li and Fung (page 38) have knowledge of local situations and may be able to help. Good transport facilities mean that even with offshoring, it may be possible to rely on just in time procedures and also adapt fast to changes in customer preferences. Careful planning is required.

Water

> **Example**
> Production methods that require natural resources such as water can be a real problem. Coca-Cola needs a lot of water for its many bottling plants. There have been serious concerns in India in the areas around the bottling plants. If water is scarce anyway, they may be depriving local people of water for drinking, household use and irrigation. This kind of issue should be addressed by local governments at the planning stage but this does not always happen. It has led to poor relationships with local people in some areas where water is scarce.

Locating within trade blocs

Trade blocs have few if any tariff barriers. Within the EU Single Market regulation is the same for all. There are opportunities to offshore production to EU economies with relatively low wage rates and skilled workforces. Portugal has a competitive advantage in certain kinds of clothing production. There are possibilities for engineering offshoring in eastern Europe.

> **Example**
> Within NAFTA, many Canadian and US companies have benefited from locating production in Mexico. A trade agreement is not the same as a common market – there is no harmonisation of regulations. But the benefits of NAFTA have been very clear and there is no evidence that producing in Mexico has reduced job opportunities in Canada or the US.

For many businesses outside a particular trade bloc, setting up subsidiaries inside the trade bloc is very important. This applies to the Japanese carmakers in the UK. After Brexit, they may move so as to stay in the EU. Equally, some UK businesses with large markets in the EU may want to manufacture in the EU rather than in the UK.

> **Think!**
> Look out for news from businesses that decide to change their locations, and consider the reasons they give. What difficulties are they likely to face?

Government incentives

One of the most significant incentives is the business tax rate. National corporation tax rates vary considerably and can be a factor in location decisions. Many companies move their headquarters to a low tax location and then arrange complex royalty payments which siphon profits off from the economy where they were earned. (Examples include Amazon, Apple, Starbucks; there are many others.) This is known as tax inversion. President Obama hoped to put a stop to it. Favourite locations in Europe are Luxembourg and Ireland. This may or may not affect the choice of location for the actual production process.

Business taxes

> **Example**
> Dell, the US computer maker, located its manufacturing operations in Limerick in the 1990s and became Ireland's largest exporter. The profits tax rate of 13% was an attraction – compared to the US rate of 30%. Then in 2009 Dell decided to cut its Limerick workforce by two thirds and move much of its production to Poland. The business tax rate there is 19% but wage costs are lower.
>
> When George Osborne cut UK corporation tax (from 28% for large business and 22% for small business in 2010 to 20% in 2016, falling to 18% in 2020) he did see the possibilities of increased FDI.

The UK government, and others among the developed and emerging economies, do provide advice to businesses considering locating in their countries. Many countries have made real efforts to simplify the process. This relates to the ease of doing business – governments that make a concerted effort to attract business are likely also to be reasonably stable. But nothing is certain!

Ease of doing business

This was largely dealt with on page 44. However, businesses that want to invest in production facilities will consider slightly different aspects of the ease of doing business from those that want to market their products or use local businesses as suppliers.

Regulations

Investors setting up their own business, either to produce or to market, will be likely to consider the number of days to start a business, local legal requirements and regulations, construction permits and energy supplies. They will also need capable local people who can help them to navigate local procedures and are bilingual or nearly so. Those that simply buy from local suppliers will be primarily concerned with trading across borders and enforcing contracts.

In China, foreign businesses that seek to produce or sell in China may be required to form a joint venture. This usually does help to get the foreign investor acquainted with Chinese business practice. It may also limit what can be achieved and misunderstandings do occur from time to time.

Political stability

Some economies that look rather unsettled but have abundant mineral resources attract investors anyway – they are taking risks but expecting a good rate of return on their investment. The oil majors in Nigeria are unlikely to be put off by occasional political instabilities.

The oil majors in Nigeria are unlikely to be put off by occasional political instabilities.

Find out

The World Bank's 'Worldwide governance indicators' can be used to compare countries. It covers six indicators that contribute to the effectiveness of governance, including political stability and absence of violence. It covers 215 countries from 1996-2014. Used in conjunction with other data noted here and in Chapter 7, you can see how a business may get in-depth information to assess individual economies. Try comparing the UK with two or three other economies.

Civil unrest

Political instability can be observed in a number of situations. There may be politically motivated violence, mass civil protest and unstable alliances between individual politicians. Opposing groups within parties may fail to agree an acceptable policy. From the business point of view, much depends on whether business leaders are able to undertake detailed and extensive assessments in advance of taking a decision.

Natural resources

Some mineral resources are located in places that would not otherwise attract multinational business, e.g. copper in the Congo, which is still suffering from recent wars and is exceptionally poor. Oil is found in many places that cannot demonstrate political stability. If the prospect of profit is sufficient, MNCs typically get around the problems, provided they can ensure that the location will not be life-threatening to their own employees. The risks will be higher but so, probably, will be the profits.

Some businesses that extract natural resources in developing countries are not careful to protect local people from the problems they create. We return to this in Chapter 15, on ethics.

Some Indian farmers are resisting giving up their farmland to make way for factories; if they lose their land they lose their incomes. This makes it difficult for Indian businesses to expand and can reduce options for FDI.

Returns on investment

Rate of return and risk

Real rates of return – the profits generated by investment – can be significantly affected by all the factors covered in this chapter. But it is never easy to forecast rates of return and there are many risks involved. Businesses need to plan for a range of possible outcomes and compare the risks associated with offshoring with the risk of doing nothing. The choice of location can be crucial so serious research work must be done. Time must be taken to evaluate the likelihood of each risk. The pros and cons of each option should be very carefully considered. Often, the highest rate of return may be expected in the riskiest location. It may make sense to accept a lower return on investment in order to reduce the risks. There is a trade-off.

Exam style question (Paper 2)

Evidence A – Offshoring

Location

AB Business Support Ltd. offers IT services to businesses and is located in Birmingham, where most of the work is currently done. Difficulties in recruiting people with the requisite skills, at reasonable rates of pay, have led the management to consider off-shoring some of their work.

AB's mangers think that work that involves liaising with customers should continue to be done in Birmingham, but much actual software development could be off-shored. They know India has good IT suppliers and think it might be worth investigating Chinese suppliers too. Recently they found information on ZDnet, a business technology news website, that Bulgaria is an increasingly attractive destination for companies thinking about outsourcing software support. There are IT specialists there who speak English; Bulgaria is within the EU and has a friendly business environment.

Your employers want you to gather information that might help them to locate a business that could undertake their routine IT development work. After some searching you have produced the data below. You explain that being able to take the business partner to court may be important if they fail to stick to the terms of their contract.

Evidence B – Data

Country	Business tax rate (%) (Deloitte)	Monthly wage ($ ppp) (ILO)	World Bank Rankings (low number best)		
			Ease of doing business	Getting electricity	Legal contract enforcing
China	25	656	84	92	7
India	30	295	130	70	178
Bulgaria	10	750	38	100	52

Questions

1. Assess the attractiveness of offshoring for AB Business Support Ltd. *(8 marks)*

2. Assess the reasons for the increase in 'reshoring'. *(10 marks)*

3. Assess the importance of tax rates when considering where to locate production. *(12 marks)*

4. Your employer has asked you to recommend a base for offshoring AB's software development. Evaluate the arguments for and against your choice. *(20 marks)*

Chapter 9
Reasons for global mergers or joint ventures

Terms to revise: organic and inorganic growth, mergers, takeovers, acquisitions and synergy (Theme 3); branding, vertical integration (Theme 3)

Bayer and Monsanto

In late 2016, Germany's massive biotech company, Bayer, completed its deal to buy Monsanto, the global leader in seeds for agriculture. The price was US$66 billion, in cash, the most expensive merger in history. The deal may not go through – both the EU and the US competition regulators will be examining the details and may decide that it cannot go ahead. The reasons are simple. Informed estimates suggest that the merged business would be selling 29% of the world's seeds and 24% of its pesticides and it could ramp up prices so that both farmers and consumers would lose some purchasing power. The Indian government protested, pointing out that there would be just three suppliers in the global market.

The reasons for merging concerned the state of the global economy. Agribusinesses were consolidating because of falling commodity prices, caused partly by the slowing of China's economic growth rate. Monsanto depended on profits from its star weed-killer, Roundup, which was used to produce weed-resistant seeds. But then the US weeds became resistant and sales fell off. The R&D department were struggling to find a good substitute but research is expensive. Innovating in a falling market is not easy.

Discussion points

Why did the companies need this merger? What consequences would it have?

Mergers

There are two ways in which a business can grow and expand. Organic growth means that the business grows from within using its own resources; it does not take over other businesses but grows by investing and expanding output and sales on its own. Inorganic growth occurs when a business gets bigger by joining with another firm, either by merger or takeover. Takeovers may simply provide useful assets. If they are kept independent they can be sold to increase liquidity if in the future the business needs cash.

Takeovers

In some ways mergers and takeovers are similar, in that they combine two previously separate businesses into a single legal entity. There is however, a difference. A merger involves the mutual decision of two companies to combine and become one entity; it can be seen as a decision made by two 'equals'. A takeover, or acquisition, on the other hand, is usually characterised by the purchase of a smaller company by a larger one. This may not be a mutual decision. A large company can initiate a hostile takeover of a smaller firm, which essentially amounts to buying the company in the face of resistance from the smaller company's management.

Many of our most familiar brand names have expanded by these means; their history can sometimes be seen in the name. GSK (GlaxoSmithKline) was the world's sixth largest pharmaceutical company as of 2015. It is a classic example of inorganic growth:

● Beechams + SmithKline Beckman = SmithKline Beecham (1989)

● Glaxo laboratories + Boroughs Wellcome = Glaxo Wellcome (1999)

● Glaxo Wellcome + SmithKline Beecham = GlaxoSmithKline!! (Some steps were missed out too.) (2000)

Joint ventures

A global alternative to inorganic growth is to enter a **joint venture** with a foreign business. This may be a one-off or temporary arrangement for a particular project, or it may be a lasting collaboration in a specific economy or market. Unlike a merger or takeover, there is no change of ownership and each joint venture will be controlled by a legal agreement drawn up between two businesses. This does not affect the operations of either business elsewhere.

> **Joint ventures** involve businesses in a collaborative relationship with a local producer. They are of particular value to businesses that want to produce and/or sell in an unfamiliar market. They can be used as a way to spread risks.

Marketing in new locations

Getting the marketing mix right usually means learning about local cultures and preferences. It is essential to recruit skilled people who know the markets that the business wants to break into. Joint ventures are a popular way of doing this, particularly in emerging markets where the foreign business may be unfamiliar with the language and culture.

Joint ventures are sometimes a government requirement for a foreign company hoping to enter a new market. This used to be the case with India and China. Although certain sectors are still safeguarded in this way, both countries now allow wholly foreign owned companies access to their markets.

Inorganic growth as a global strategy

Economies of scale

There are many reasons why mergers and takeovers occur and they are often interlinked. Bayer and Monsanto were looking for economies of scale to help pay for expensive research. Procter and Gamble (P&G) bought Gillette in 2005, in a deal worth $57 billion, to become the world's biggest household goods maker, pushing Unilever into second place. This was not done just to grow, increase market share and make more profit. It removed a major competitor and gave P&G access to Gillette's important and lucrative portfolio of brand names. Between them, they share 21 brands that each have annual sales of more than $1bn. Not only that, their grooming brands complement each other; P&G specialises in hair and skincare for women, while Gillette focuses on male grooming. The deal also yielded cost savings of between $14bn and $16bn from economies of scale and internal restructuring.

Reaching larger markets

Heineken

In early 2010 Heineken, one of the world's largest brewers, launched a successful takeover of the Mexican group, Femsa Cerveza, which had 14 breweries in Mexico and Brazil. Among their brands were Sol and Dos Equis. It was almost exactly two years since Heineken, along with Carlsberg, had taken over Scottish & Newcastle breweries in the UK. Since then, the British beer market had declined, a combination of the smoking ban, the recession and a series of duty increases doing much to reduce trade. Heineken found it tough going.

The €5.3 billion (£4.8 billion) takeover of Femsa Cerveza gave Heineken a big foothold in Mexico, one of the world's most profitable beer markets. Mexico sells most of its beer through what one might generously call convenience stores. While some of these 300,000 outlets are proper shops, most are 'mom and pop' affairs that are little more than private houses with a kiosk on the side where customers knock for service. This may sound primitive but, unlike Britain, Mexico's market for beer is still growing.

By taking over Femsa, Heineken has improved the balance of earnings from mature and emerging markets – the latter now account for 40 per cent – and has also maintained Heineken's position as a global force. Heineken said that it expected the annual cost savings to reach €150 million by 2013.

In 2015 Heineken continued to expand by taking over Slovenian brewer Pivovarna Lasko for €120 million. Then it bought the Jamaican company Desnoes & Geddes, in a €696 million deal, to boost its presence in the Caribbean. The next takeover was of Malaysian brewer GAB, producers of such beers as Tiger, Anchor and Malta.

1. Explain as many reasons as you can why Heineken might have wanted to takeover Femsa Cerveza.

2. Explain why improving "the balance of earnings from mature and emerging markets" may be important to Heineken.

3. Assess the impact on Mexican consumers and local businesses of Heineken's takeover.

4. Evaluate the likely role of mergers and takeovers in Heineken's international success.

Spreading risk over different countries or regions

As a global company expands by mergers and takeovers it builds up a portfolio of businesses. These may be similar to the main business or completely different in both nature and location. This provides both balance and stability in a global company. Having operations in different economies means that a downturn in one country is not as serious as it might be; other markets may be doing well. These are known as 'risk-bearing economies of scale'. For example, Heineken in the case study were looking for growth in emerging markets such as Mexico and Brazil, to balance out the falling beer sales in western markets such as the UK.

As a global company expands by mergers and takeovers it builds up a portfolio of businesses.

Diversified markets

Diversified products

Eastman Kodak, long famous for its cameras and photographic films, experienced a severe downturn with the advent of digital photography. To a certain extent it offset this by moving into digital photography but it has also moved into different fields through mergers and takeovers. Amongst others, it bought NuPro Technologies, which make cleaners and lubricants for the printer industry, in 2008. In 2010 it bought Laser-Pacific Media which provides a variety of video postproduction services, primarily for television shows. Heineken grew by diversifying into new markets while Eastman Kodak survived by diversifying into different products. Risks can be spread and uncertainty reduced by mergers and takeovers.

Entering new markets and trade blocs

Inorganic growth

Businesses that want to launch into a new market can choose between setting up distributors that will sell their exports, entering into a joint venture, taking over a local company or setting up their own production facilities. All require some preparation – even just exporting successfully will usually require market research. Joint ventures and building production facilities both require engagement with local people and willingness to explore cultural issues. Taking over a business that is active in the target market can be the simplest and most convenient way for a global business to get a foothold and build a presence in that market.

Merging with or taking over a foreign business can be a difficult process, fraught with unforeseen problems. Taking over an existing business reduces uncertainty. Supply chains and distribution networks are already in place and consumers are familiar with existing brands. This can be particularly important where markets are expanding rapidly and there is little or no time to enter and grow by organic means. Mergers and takeovers enable businesses to keep pace with dynamic markets. Sometimes entering new markets is the only way to expand, as the established domestic markets may be saturated or even in decline. Such was the case with Heineken in the case study above.

> **Example**
> Refresco Group, Europe's largest soft drinks bottler, took over US-based bottler Whitlock Packaging for £98m in 2016. Refresco has established its leading position in Europe over the past 16 years through the successful strategy of buying and building. This latest acquisition enables Refresco to enter the lucrative North American market for the first time.

A similar logic applies to entering a trade bloc. By taking over or merging with another business it can then use that as a base from which to access the markets in the rest of the trade bloc, without any trade restrictions.

Patents

Brand acquisition

Example

Mayer Brown JSM, a leading law company that operates in Hong Kong, China and many ASEAN economies, has managed to get round protectionist restrictions and access the Chinese market by forming a joint venture with Jingtian & Gongcheng. The firms will operate as separate entities but with joint legal teams and shared office space.

Acquiring national and international brand names and patents

Brands can be very important for global businesses; they already have an established image and loyal customers. In many cases when one business is taking over another, the brand is worth more than the physical assets that go with it. Not only that, but a readymade market segment comes with it. For a business that does not operate in that particular segment, this is a useful and rapid way of expanding market share and reaching more consumers.

All the initial expense and time involved in creating a brand from scratch can be avoided by buying the business that owns it. Similarly, a business may take over a business that has a valuable patent. The patent system exists to encourage innovation; patented products or processes cannot be copied by competing businesses, usually for 20 years. The price of a takeover deal that involves a patent will reflect the effort and expense of the innovation process.

> **Patents** are legal rights to a monopoly on a new product or process. The innovator applies to the Patent Office. Once the patent is obtained, the holder can manufacture the product or licence other businesses to produce it. Businesses that copy the patented product illegally can be challenged in the courts.

Show your understanding

Since the 80s L'Oréal, the world's largest cosmetics company, has pursued a successful programme of expansion by acquiring brands that both increase and complement its existing product portfolio. The brand names are important and are kept on, despite now being owned by another company. L'Oréal has transformed itself from an exclusively French company, narrowly focused on white women, into a global business whose skin, hair and cosmetics products are tailored to consumers all over the world. For example, in 1998 and 2000 it acquired Softsheen and Carson. These companies provided beauty products for the African American ethnic market in the USA.

Since then L'Oréal has built on this and used these brands to penetrate other markets such as South Africa. To speed up their expansion in China, L'Oréal acquired Mininurse, a Chinese mass skin-care brand, in 2003. In 2004 they bought Shu Uemura, a Japanese cosmetics firm. In 2006 it took over The Body Shop and in 2012 went a step further and took over Urban Decay, a specialist American company that is vegan and does not use any animal products at all. In 2014 it acquired Magic Holdings, a Hong Kong based facial care brand, to help maintain its dominance in the Chinese market. These are just some of the businesses acquired by L'Oréal, which seems to have a gift for identifying major growth areas, looking at the leading brands and then moving in.

1. Identify two other businesses that have pursued a similar strategy.

2. What are the advantages of this approach?

3. Why do L'Oréal keep their brands distinct from one another?

4. How can L'Oréal have grown so big without appearing to encounter diseconomies of scale?

Securing resources and supplies

When a business operates on a global scale, its supply chain can be long and at times uncertain. Relying on other businesses to keep you supplied with necessary inputs can be a problem, particularly if there is also a strong competitor that is also trying to obtain those supplies. Costs may increase and production may be uncertain. To get round this problem some businesses will take over the supplier to ensure that they will always be able to obtain resources at a reasonable cost. This process is called backwards vertical integration.

Backwards vertical integration

French luxury goods maker Chanel has just bought four silk suppliers to strengthen its supply chain. This follows other acquisitions of suppliers in recent years such as feather providers, milliners and boot-makers. Chanel's competitors, including Hermes, Kering, Richemont and LVMH, have also been buying suppliers, from tanneries to flower growers. They are securing access to high quality raw materials for which there is fierce competition. Bringing the suppliers into the business not only reduces costs and risks, but also deprives the competition of a possible source of supply.

> **Example**
> At the time of writing (2016) the electronics manufacturing giant Foxconn of Taiwan is bidding to acquire the Japanese electronics company Sharp. Foxconn's biggest customer is Apple and Sharp makes some of the iDevices screens, and has some highly advanced mobile screen technologies. By owning Sharp, Foxconn could have greater control over the supply of the components it assembles into Apple products, as well as expanding into production rather than just contract manufacturing and assembly.

Maintaining and increasing global competitiveness

As markets expand and become more open and global, some businesses may get left behind or have difficulty in keeping pace with the leading companies. A merger may help to maintain or increase competitiveness. BA (British Airways) and Iberia, Spain's national carrier, announced plans to merge at the end of 2009. The merger allowed the company to compete more effectively with other European giants, including Air France-KLM and Germany's Lufthansa. At the time US Airways and United Airlines were also planning to merge and form a larger competitor on a worldwide basis. Of course these mergers were not just to do with keeping up with the competition; they were also influenced by the pressures of the 2008-12 recession and a downturn in the number of passengers.

Market share

Market share can be expanded rapidly by inorganic growth in the form of mergers and takeovers; this is particularly important in some of today's rapidly expanding global markets. For most global industries, the driving force is the profit motive. Increased market share means more sales, greater revenue and hopefully more profit. This rewards shareholders and management, and enables further investment and growth to take place.

One of the primary objectives is to reduce average costs by achieving economies of scale. Falling costs can lead to reduced prices and a competitive advantage, or higher profits. These can be re-invested for more growth. In competitive global markets this can be all important.

Re-structuring

When two companies come together, there is often duplication of resources. They may no longer need two head offices or two distribution depots. By disposing of surplus resources savings can be made and efficiency increased. Unfortunately for some people this re-structuring or rationalisation means that they lose their jobs. The P&G takeover of Gillette saw 6,000 jobs cut from the new, larger business.

Synergy

Synergy is an added something that can be gained when two businesses join together. It comes from the Greek 'synergia', which means joint work and cooperative action. The word is used quite often to mean that combining forces produces a better product or business. For example a merger of two oil companies, one with a superior distribution network and the other with more reserves, would have synergy and would be expected to result in higher earnings per share than previously.

> **Synergy** is the idea that after a merger or takeover, the performance of a combined enterprise will exceed that of its previously separate parts. Sometimes this is expressed as 2 + 2 = 5.

Poundland, the retail chain, was taken over in 2016 by Steinhoff, a major global retailer based in South Africa.

How effective are mergers and acquisitions?

Merger and takeover outcomes

Mergers and takeovers actually have a poor track record of success. Although the idea might look good on paper, less than 50% are estimated to deliver the anticipated benefits. There are several main reasons for this. Mostly it is the human element that gets the blame: different organisations can be very difficult to join together. There can be clashes of corporate cultures and management styles, and the workforce may be suspicious of change. There is also the danger that businesses become too spread out and move away from their core strengths. Mergers and takeovers tend to follow the economic cycle and increase when the economy is booming, but when times are hard many fall apart. A glance in the business section of the press will often show large numbers of firms selling off parts of their business (divestment). For every success story such as Procter and Gamble or L'Oréal, there is a Rover and BMW or Time AOL and Warner. Synergy may fail to appear.

Exam style question (Paper 3)

Poundland, the retail chain, was taken over in 2016 by Steinhoff, a major global retailer based in South Africa. Poundland has around 18,000 staff spread across more than 900 stores in the UK, Ireland and Spain. Its HQ is in Willenhall, near Wolverhampton.

Steinhoff has over 6,500 outlets in 30 countries and owns over 40 retail brands including Bensons for Beds and Harveys in the UK, Conforama in Europe, Pep, Ackermans and Hardware Warehouse in South Africa and Snooze in Australia. Its 2011 acquisition of the French homeware retailer, Conforama, brought six new countries into the group's control.

Steinhoff has pursued an expansionary strategy based on mergers and takeovers. In its latest set of results, operating profit had jumped 46% to $1.2bn in the nine months to March 2016, compared with the same period the year before.

1. Explain two reasons why Steinhoff may have wanted to take over Poundland. *(8 marks)*

2. Assess the impact this may have on Poundland and its employees. *(10 marks)*

3. Assess the benefits that an international business such as Steinhoff may achieve from expansion. *(12 marks)*

4. Using the evidence and other examples in this chapter, evaluate the likely consequences of inorganic growth for a range of international businesses. *(20 marks)*

Chapter 10

Global competitiveness

Terms to revise: exchange rate changes (Theme 2); price elasticities (Theme 1); competitive advantage.

Trade, prices and exchange rates

Changing exchange rates

Table 1 shows what happened to a range of exchange rates against the US dollar between mid-2014 and mid-2015. The figures show the cost of a US$ in terms of the national currency. Interesting things were happening in the world economy at the time.

Table 1: Exchange rates, selected economies, value of US$1, 2014-15

	July 2014	**July 2015**
UK £	0.58	0.65
Eurozone €	0.73	0.90
Japan yen	102	121
China renminbi	6.20	6.21
Russia rouble	34.2	57.5

Source: Bank of England

All the currencies in the table fell against the dollar. The price of a dollar rose for each one of them. Imports from the US cost more in 2015 than they did in 2014. Obviously the dollar was rising in value.

The reasons are easy to find. Oil and gas recently discovered in the mid-west and US expertise in fracking, meant that many countries could get cheaper energy from the USA. US exports rose. The importers bought dollars to pay for the extra oil and gas, pushing the price of the dollar upwards. For the UK, the £ was worth less; it would take more pounds to buy dollars.

The more world oil supplies rose, the further the oil price fell. Russia is a big exporter of oil and gas; it relies heavily on its export revenue. Russia had to cut its oil and gas prices, to stay competitive. The buyers could get the oil and gas they needed with fewer roubles.

Questions

1. For the UK and the Eurozone, work out how much more a tourist going to the USA would have to pay for US$100, in 2015, compared to 2014. (Answer on page 107.)

2. How would a hotel in Paris feel about the exchange rate change? (Paris is a popular destination for US tourists.)

3. How would a Parisian who likes to visit New York feel?

4. Work out what happened to the revenue Russia received for its exports of oil and gas.

Most economies have **floating exchange rates**. Exchange rates fluctuate, depending on the supply and demand for the currency. There is a constant flow of buyers and sellers: foreign buyers of UK-produced goods and services (UK exports, including tourism) will want to buy UK pounds. Sellers of UK pounds will be people and businesses that need to buy foreign currencies to pay for imports (including tourism abroad).

The euro

The Eurozone works a little differently. The euro itself has a floating exchange rate. But inside the Eurozone, the 19 member countries have adopted the single currency and their exchange rate is effectively fixed for all trading with each other. Their governments cannot change it or let their exchange rate float to a different level. The euro is useful for many UK exporters and importers because it saves them from having to deal in 19 different currencies.

Appreciation

When the exchange rate is rising, it appreciates. If the demand for pounds to pay for UK exports is rising, it will push up the value of the pound, which will appreciate on the foreign exchange market.

Similarly, if people in the UK are buying fewer imports, the supply of pounds will fall because less foreign currency is needed to pay for imports. On the foreign exchange market the pound becomes scarcer. The exchange rate rises and the pound appreciates.

Depreciation

When the exchange rate is falling, it depreciates. If UK exports are falling, fewer pounds will be demanded to pay for the exports. As with anything else, if less is required, prices fall. The pound will be worth less; it depreciates on the foreign exchange market.

Similarly, if people in the UK are buying more imports, the supply of pounds will increase as more foreign currency is needed to pay for the imports. The pound becomes more plentiful and depreciates.

Capital flows

The level of a **floating exchange rate** is determined by market forces. It reflects the demand for the currency, to buy its products or invest there, and the supply of the currency, which arises from its buying imports and capital flows abroad.

Appreciation refers to rising value. When the pound appreciates, a pound buys more of another currency than it did before. Importers' competitive advantage increases.

Depreciation means falling values. When the pound depreciates, a pound buys less of another currency than it did before. The competitive advantage of exporters is increased.

Competitive advantage

The impact of movement in exchange rates

Movements in exchange rates can affect the competitiveness of businesses. An appreciation helps importers but disadvantages exporters. A depreciation has the opposite effect.

Appreciation
- Appreciation is generally seen as being bad for exporters; it makes them less competitive. Foreign buyers have to give up more of their own currency to buy the exports and demand may fall.

- Importers tend to benefit as they need to spend less of their own currency, thus increasing profitability or giving them the chance to lower prices and increase their competitive advantage.

- Consumers may respond by buying more imports but this may reduce the sales of domestic competitors.

- Businesses that rely on imports for raw materials or components are likely to see a fall in their costs of production.

Depreciation
- Exporters are likely to find depreciation a good thing because it makes them more competitive. The price at which they sell in foreign markets can be cut. Buyers need to exchange less currency and so demand may increase boosting sales and competitiveness. Exporters have a choice: they may cut prices in foreign currency, or leave them the same and make a bigger profit.

Export choices

- Importers are less happy as they must now exchange more of their own currency to make purchases and this reduces profitability. They may have to accept this in order to maintain sales or they may increase their prices to compensate.

- Domestic producers may benefit as consumers move away from the now more expensive imported products.

- Businesses that import raw materials or components will see a rise in their costs of production.

Business options

Some businesses will not be affected by changing exchange rates, either directly or indirectly. The exchange rate influences most directly those businesses involved in international trade. The size of the impact depends upon a range of factors such as the degree to which the business is involved in trade, the size of the exchange rate movement and its duration, the nature of the product or service involved and the price elasticity of demand of the products concerned.

Show your understanding

1. You run the finance department of Absolute, a business that manufactures electricity generators and imports special batteries from Germany. The exchange rate is £1 = €1.20. You know you need to buy €50,000 to pay for the latest consignment of batteries. What will it cost you in £s?

2. The £ depreciates to €1.15 before you get around to buying the euros you need. How much more will you have to pay, in £s? (Answers on page 107.)

3. Your line manager is furious. You can look around for batteries produced in the UK. Or you can look for imported batteries from outside the Eurozone. Or you can suggest to the marketing department that they increase the price of your generators. Your biggest customers are UK hospitals that need generators in case of power cuts. Discuss the pros and cons of each strategy and decide how to put your proposal to the line manager.

The significance of price elasticities

Price elasticity of demand is important here. If the pound depreciates it may have relatively little impact on the demand for oil, which is price inelastic. But it may cause many consumers to buy holidays in the UK rather than go abroad. The price elasticity of demand for foreign holidays is much higher than it is for oil. The price elasticity of demand for generators for hospitals will depend upon the availability of similar products from other sources. Similarly, if the pound depreciates, a UK exporter of a patented component for gear boxes may be able to raise its prices by the amount of the depreciation and still sell the goods, provided their product really is very superior to all the competing substitutes.

How buyers react

Show your understanding

1. If there are good substitutes for the generators that are made in the UK, what will this tell you about the price elasticity of demand for the generators?

2. How will it affect the decision about how to react to the exchange rate depreciation?

3. What will a chain of off-licences do if depreciation raises the cost of a bottle of wine?

4. How will Jaguar Land Rover react to an appreciation of the pound?

All exchange rate changes take time to have an effect. Some take longer than others – appreciation may cause import prices to rise quite quickly. But exporters need time to gear up to higher levels of production as exchange rates depreciate. It can take as long as two years to see the full effects of an exchange rate change.

Competitive advantage

Most businesses strive to achieve a competitive advantage. Potential strategies for achieving a competitive advantage include:

- seeking out low cost production locations (offshoring) or suppliers who can cut the cost of certain processes of inputs (outsourcing).
- entering new markets when existing markets are saturated.

Innovation

- developing any product feature that leads to an advantage over rival products, based on price, quality, service, reputation, innovation or any other source of differentiation.
- cutting costs through lean production or other process innovations.

These strategies are just as important in a global market as they are in a domestic one. Cost competitiveness and differentiation are two key ways to achieve global competitiveness.

Cost competitiveness

Economies of scale

Economies of scale: any successful business pays close attention to its costs but globalisation has enabled some international businesses to expand and take advantage of new economies of scale. Lower average costs mean that selling prices can be reduced; in a mass market, this can lead to increased sales and market share.

> **Example**
> Walmart is able to achieve economies of scale in many ways such as bulk buying and mass marketing. It is also able to dictate terms to its supplier companies to minimise costs. As a result Walmart has become known for its cheap prices, which give it a competitive advantage on a global scale. In 2015 its global sales were $482.1 billion.
>
> Besides the global giants, many smaller businesses can pursue a low cost strategy. In the UK the rise of the discount food retailers such as Aldi and Lidl is based on their low cost model; they have been so successful that the other supermarkets are having to adapt.

Productivity can be increased with a range of strategies that enhance efficiency:

- Better training makes employees more capable and therefore more productive.

Lean production

- Automation or using the most appropriate technologies can cut labour costs.
- Innovation through careful management reduces waste – think of lean production or lean management.

Offshoring can cut labour costs.

> In 2015 the Japanese electronics company Panasonic Corp announced that it would close its lithium-ion battery factory in Beijing and cut 1,300 jobs. Taiwan's Foxconn, the handset manufacturer for brands such as Apple, is investing $5 billion in building assembly plants in India. Samsung is investing an additional US$3 billion in Vietnam, to increase its existing facilities.

Outsourcing as Nike does, with its policy of using independent businesses in South East Asia to manufacture its products, reduces costs because all employees including managers will be paid at local rates. Many other suppliers of clothing and footwear do the same.

Cost leadership – essentially a pricing strategy – usually involves targeting the market segments that are most price-sensitive. This works well where a business has products that offer very good value for money but may not be clearly differentiated from rival products, except by price and perhaps style. These products will appeal to many people with limited spending power. (Of course you could conceivably achieve cost leadership by selling the cheapest diamond rings.)

Cost leadership

One of the problems of pursuing a low cost strategy is that rivals can soon catch up by adopting similar tactics. China's growth in recent decades has been fueled by more and more businesses seeking lower manufacturing costs. In order to remain competitive some businesses are now leaving China and seeking out lower cost bases. Examples include Panasonic and Foxconn.

Low cost strategies

Differentiation

While controlling cost is important for any business, some choose a different route to competitive advantage, through non-price competition. This is ideal for businesses that cannot compete solely on price in any market. They can add value in a whole range of ways that enable them to sell at a higher price.

Non-price competition

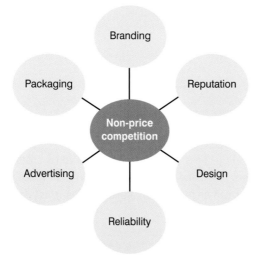

Branding and reputation – where it is possible, a business may build a brand reputation to differentiate itself from its rivals. It doesn't matter if the difference is real or perceived. If customers appreciate the difference they will be prepared to pay a premium price for the product or service. The effectiveness of branding can be enhanced by careful market research.

Branding

Design and reliability are very significant differentiating factors. Design provides a visible message that can be a part of personal identity. Reliability appeals to the practicality of customers who look for lasting value for money and low risk of product failure.

Marketing style can be sufficient on its own to differentiate a product. Coca-Cola has dominated the global cola market by advertising itself as a lifestyle product. Businesses that target very specific market segments can hone their advertising to appeal to specific groups of people. Some businesses use their style of packaging to differentiate their product.

Packaging

International businesses such as BMW, Apple and L'Oréal are all examples of businesses pursuing a differentiation strategy. At the same time their global reach gives them the opportunity to take advantage of economies of scale so that they can both charge premium prices and increase their profitability.

Creating a competitive advantage by differentiation is not easy. Brands and reputations are hard, not to mention, expensive to create. A business will need to innovate constantly and promote to maintain its reputation.

Brand loyalty

Recruitment problems

Skill shortages and international competitiveness

The UK has a persistent problem of skill shortages. Even during a recession, some skills remain scarce. Businesses experience this as difficulty in recruiting people with the skills they require. They may need to replace people who are retiring, or to expand their activities. Governments have been concerned about this for some time but neither politicians nor business people have given sufficient attention to the need for additional training.

This affects competitiveness because businesses that are constantly struggling to recruit have to increase rates of pay in order to get the people they want. Unfilled vacancies make it difficult to meet demand and higher pay means higher costs. Some businesses find themselves having to turn away export orders; others find that with the staff they have, they cannot meet delivery deadlines. Other businesses may fail to make full use of new technologies.

The government keeps a list of scarce skills which is used to decide which people can be granted visas to work in the UK. The list includes many types of engineers, digital technology and cyber security experts, farm workers and health care professionals. Also, many construction companies are short of people with specific skills, including, currently, bricklayers.

Airbus, Rolls Royce and other major exporters have complained strongly about skill shortages. Airbus said: "*currently there is a genuine lack of people within the resident labour market capable of filling certain positions and recruitment from overseas is absolutely essential if Airbus is to both retain a competitive edge and be able to recruit the best qualified people in this field.*"

Many construction companies are short of people with specific skills.

Improving training

Why don't businesses have training schemes to fill the gaps? Training is expensive and eats into profits. It ties up experienced staff and trainees may work slowly or make mistakes for some time before they become both fully qualified and experienced. It is far cheaper to recruit capable people from overseas, or poach people from rival companies, with promises of high pay and perks.

Businesses that compete on price will not be able to increase prices to cover the costs associated with skill shortages. They are likely to have wafer-thin profit margins. So there will be little cash available to fund investment in training or higher pay that could attract new recruits.

A new government policy

In early 2016, the then Chancellor of the Exchequer, George Osborne, wheeled out a new policy for apprenticeship training. The scheme would require a payroll tax, to be paid by businesses with annual wage bills over £3 million, amounting to 0.5% of the wage bill. Altogether it would generate revenue of £11 billion. In return for the tax, businesses would get vouchers to cover the training costs. In effect this would force them to set up training programmes.

There was uproar. The CBI (Confederation of British Industries) protested and many businesses were bitterly opposed to the scheme. But in August 2016, Prime Minister May announced that the scheme would go ahead in 2017, despite all the objections. The programme would create three million new apprenticeships by 2020. Some sensible concessions were made: companies would be allowed to claim for the costs of retraining existing staff and would get funding for higher levels of advanced skills training (i.e. additional training for graduates).

As of 2016, many businesses had retained profits sitting in their banks. There have been cuts in funding for further education colleges, which have a significant role in training schemes.

Think!

Why would businesses be so unwilling to provide adequate training schemes? Why might the government have cut funding to further education?

Chapter 11

Marketing

Terms to revise: the marketing mix; Ansoff's Matrix (Theme 3).

Differentiated products

Global marketing strategy and global localisation (glocalisation)

KitKat has been adapted for sale all over the world. In Russia, it is slightly smaller and the chocolate is coarser than elsewhere. In the USA it has added sugar and less milk in the chocolate. In Malaysia it is produced in a special formula for warm climates. In Japan it comes in a bewildering array of over 300 flavours including wasabi, purple sweet potato, maple syrup, grape, apple, banana, kiwifruit, azuki, green tea, yuzu, cherry blossom and even sake. Peter Brabeck, Chairman of Nestlé, said *"Each of these product variations is the result of thorough market research on local tastes. There is no global consumer for the food-and-beverage business."*

Discussion point

Why is it worthwhile for Nestlé to differentiate its products to this extent?

Adaptation

Global marketing involves applying conventional marketing strategies but for a range of different markets – some of which are very different indeed. Some businesses study their markets very carefully and adapt their product to each one. Others trade on the uniqueness of their brand, specifically to gain from the reputation it already has. In contrast to Nestlé, Coca-Cola and Pepsi stick closely to their traditional recipes, having a clear corporate and global brand identity that is the same the world over. However, they do vary their promotional activities to suit local markets. KitKat's range of flavours for the Japanese market shows the alternative approach, aiming to cater for local market preferences.

> **Global marketing** refers to the marketing strategies used by businesses when operating in global markets. The elements of the marketing mix may be the same or varied to suit a particular part of the global market.

'Think global, act local'

This saying has been applied to many fields of work but in the business sense it can be described as achieving globalisation while remaining locally accountable. It highlights the importance of operating on a global basis but paying attention to the needs and wants of each individual market at the same time. The approach can be adapted to enhance reputations and develop profitable strategies.

Example

In India, one of Coca-Cola's advertisements featured Bollywood star Hrithik Roshan. A group of youngsters go out for a late night snack, only to find the eateries shut. They meet Hrithik on the way and go on a magical midnight tryst with the star. Coca-Cola adds the fizz. This advert is aimed at India's students and young professionals who are looking for a bit of excitement in the globalised environment.

Glocalisation

This approach is sometimes called **glocalisation**, a saleable mix of the global and the local. The term was first used by social scientist Manfred Lange in 1989 on the eve of the Global Change Exhibition in Moscow.

Glocalisation combines the words 'globalisation' and 'localisation' to emphasise the idea that a global product or service is more likely to succeed if it is adapted to the specific requirements of local practices and cultural expectations.

Example

Disney opened its first theme park in mainland China in June 2016. The park in Shanghai does not just copy the American version but adds elements that will appeal to Chinese visitors by incorporating Chinese stories, history, symbolism and local customs.

There is a peony flower design on the turret of the park's centerpiece castle, a Beijing opera interlude in the Mandarin version of the Lion King musical and the Shanghai park castle was designed with eating and retail space inside to meet Chinese expectations.

"We didn't build Disneyland in China, we built China's Disneyland," said Disney Chief Executive Officer Robert Iger.

There are two opposing views that a business can adopt when considering a global marketing strategy. Alternatively, the two can be combined to form a third.

The domestic approach (Ethnocentric Model)

A standardised marketing mix

Some firms tend to transfer their existing domestic business model to the international arena. They see foreign markets as identical to their domestic markets. If it works at home, it will work over there. There is no necessity to change the design of the product, nor any of the associated marketing activities. The marketing mix can be standardised, allowing the company to reap marketing economies of scale as it expands production. It can minimise the amount of time and resources devoted to individual markets. This may help to reduce average costs and give the firm a competitive advantage, but they risk losing sales because their marketing mix is not oriented to individual markets.

Ethnocentric Model: an approach to marketing whereby the business approaches the world primarily from the perspective of its own culture. It assumes that what was a success story in the domestic market will also be so in the other economies where it operates. Foreign operations are treated as secondary or subordinate to the domestic market. Products and services are sold without adaptation.

The international approach (Polycentric Model)

Customised marketing

There can be significant social and cultural differences in doing business between countries. For many firms, operating on a global basis means that they will need to adapt some parts of their marketing mix to maximise sales in different markets. Some businesses take this approach to extremes and develop a unique marketing mix for each market's individual characteristics. Every market is seen as distinctive; products and marketing activities (distribution, promotion and price) are all individually customised. This usually results in sales increases on a local basis but sometimes at the expense of profit. Customisation inevitably results in increased costs; it reduces the marketing economies of scale because each market needs individual attention.

There can be significant social and cultural differences in doing business between countries.

Polycentric Model: an approach that considers each host country to be unique. Subsidiary businesses develop their own individual business and marketing strategies in order to suit these particular needs.

The mixed approach (Geocentric Model)

Mixing approaches

Some businesses enjoy a happy medium. They get some of the advantages of a standardised approach, reaping economies of scale, but also cater for the needs of individual markets in order to maximise sales. More sophisticated multinationals recognise this and organise their marketing in a way that is sometimes described as the modularisation of marketing. The idea is simple: what needs to be managed globally is organised in one way while local needs are managed in other ways. In consumer markets, this tends to mean that concepts or platforms e.g. the brand and global identity, are managed globally. Smaller markets are a local responsibility and adapt accordingly.

Geocentric approach sees the whole world as a potential market but with both similarities and differences in domestic and foreign markets. An effort is made to develop integrated world market strategies to gain the best from both of these strands.

McDonalds

By 2016 McDonald's had 36,538 restaurants worldwide in 119 different countries. Clearly, with this kind of distribution, the demographic variations are enormous. For many years, McDonald's menus were entirely standardised. But during the 1990s, the company seemed to lose its dynamism and had a rethink. It moved into an ongoing process of adapting restaurants and menus to cater for the types of people who are most likely to be customers in each individual economy. While its main focus would still be on burgers, it started to offer salads and vegetarian items as well as locally popular foods.

Local specialities

There are many diverse influences to be catered for. In India, for example, the cow is a sacred animal for many Hindus and so they developed the Maharajah Mac which uses chicken rather than beef. In Saudi Arabia no pork products are served as it is prohibited by Islamic law. All meat sold is halal. In Israel there are both kosher and non-kosher branches. Differing tastes lead to a large variety of offerings so if you fancy a McSpaghetti – spaghetti noodles served in sweet tomato-based sauce, with hot dogs and grated pasteurised cheese – go to the Philippines. In south Korea try the McBingsoo (a Patbingsu sweet dessert with shaved ice), in Singapore try fish McDippers or the McSpicy. In Malaysia a bestseller is Bubur Ayam McD which literally translates as 'chicken porridge'. In Japan you can accompany your Teri Tama Burger or Ebi Filet-O with seaweed flavoured french fries.

Standardised marketing

Despite all of this regional variety, the familiar golden arches with the red and yellow colour schemes of McDonald's can be seen almost all over the world. The strength and identity of the global brand gives them a real competitive advantage and sends a clear signal to consumers everywhere. Yet it takes great care to tailor its products to individual market tastes, maximising sales. Love them or loathe them, this really is a business that follows the 'Think global, act local' message.

1. What evidence can you find to support the idea that McDonald's have a geocentric approach to their marketing?

2. Can you think of any disadvantages of McDonald's marketing strategies?

3. "There is no global consumer for the food-and-beverage business." (Peter Brabeck) To what extent do you agree with this statement?

Whilst it may be relatively straightforward for a company like McDonald's to adapt its products and marketing strategy to suit a number of different markets, other companies may struggle. In an industry such as consumer electronics, characterised by high product development costs and rapidly changing

Japanese companies such as Sony and Panasonic have been successful in marketing standardised versions of their products.

Standardised products

technology, there is a real need for developing globally standardised products and services. By serving large markets, development costs can be quickly recovered. There are significant economies of scale. Japanese companies such as Sony and Panasonic have been successful in marketing standardised versions of their products. Many of Sony's consumer electronics products are highly standardised except for the parts that meet national electrical standards. Apple with their iconic range of products follows a similar strategy.

Applying the marketing mix (4Ps) to global markets

What all of these companies are doing is using the marketing mix just as you might expect, but adjusting it to a greater or lesser degree to fit the circumstances. We have seen how products can be changed to suit the local market, as with McDonald's, or not, as with Sony and Apple.

Price is a crucial part of successful marketing in a global context. For some markets price will need to be low to attract customers. The level of economic development may not permit standard western pricing tactics. The fast food companies moving into India know this and always have some low price items on their menus. Levi Strauss has developed a lightweight pair of jeans for use in the monsoon season in India. They are expensive at 9,000 rupees but they dry out fast and Levi's have developed a 'pay-as-you-wear' scheme, so that buyers can pay in installments.

Adapting to local incomes

Product: as we have seen, the actual product can undergo a wide variety of permutations and adaptations to suit local tastes. This is particularly true for food and drink but also for other products. When Nike produces a sports clothing range it may stay the same in terms of design but different size ranges are produced to suit different countries. People in SE Asia are generally smaller than Europeans. Jaguar motor cars modify the rear of their cars for the Chinese market because many buyers employ chauffeurs and so the luxury is concentrated on the rear seats.

Promotion is also tailored to suit local tastes and interests. Coca-Cola, is a good example here, with its links to the Bollywood star (page 65), who is virtually unknown in the west. The Future Group in India is a chain of supermarkets that uses traditional ways of selling its products. Not for them the ordered and neat rows of products. Their displays are deliberately disorganised and live up to the idea of 'organised chaos'. This is because many Indian consumers are distrustful of neat, tidy displays because they suggest high

Appropriate distribution

prices. So their promotional displays are intended to mimic the traditional chaotic bazaars and kiranas (corner shops).

Place: in many parts of developing nations the infrastructure that we take for granted in countries like the UK may not be present. Businesses have to come up with other solutions if they are to penetrate these markets. When the roads run out in countries such as Tanzania, Coca-Cola use a lorry to deliver to an MDC (Manual Distribution Center), often an entrepreneur with a storage container, who will take the entire load. Distribution from the MDCs is then mostly by hand with crates being loaded on to handcarts, bicycles and anything else that can be used to reach the remote villages.

Market penetration

Place and promotion are neatly combined by Unilever's Shakti Programme, which helps women in rural India to set up small businesses as direct-to-consumer retailers. The scheme equips women with business skills and a way out of poverty, as well as creating a crucial new distribution channel for Unilever products. This means that their products now reach millions of potential new customers in rural areas, where no one would previously have been able to access them. By 2015 the Shakti network had reached 165,000 villages with over 4 million households. They are now creating similar schemes in Egypt, Nigeria, Sri Lanka and Pakistan.

> **Nestlé in Africa**
>
> In 2008 Nestlé began work on an investment programme across 21 countries in equatorial Africa. The company was banking on the expected growth of middle class consumers. In the oil exporting countries – Nigeria, Sudan and Angola, a significant middle class is emerging. Nigeria is thought to have 8 million middle class households already, forecast to reach 21 million by 2030. Nestlé's efforts there have been worthwhile. However, in Kenya, a very different situation has emerged. Two thirds of Nairobi's residents live in informal settlements. (This is a polite description of shanty towns, some of which are slums.) Nestlé is not doing well there because local companies are fighting back. They have local appeal and have put time and money into raising product standards and creating their own brands, tailored to suit local people. Regional supermarket chains are creating their own cheap and reliable brands. They are competing successfully with Nestlé. UK brand Weetabix, now owned by China, thinks it has 80% of the Kenyan cereal market.
>
> 1. Using the terminology on pages 66-7 how would you describe Nestlé's approach?
>
> 2. How might Nestlé have used the 4Ps to help create a viable strategy for Kenya?

Applying Ansoff's matrix to global markets

Strategies for global growth

Ansoff's matrix is a tool designed to highlight the elements of a business strategy that will lead to growth and the development of a successful product portfolio. It divides a business on the basis of both the products it has, or could have, and the markets it is already in, or could be in. The four quadrants can be used to guide a business that is about to enter international markets or one that is already operating there.

Figure 1: Ansoff's matrix

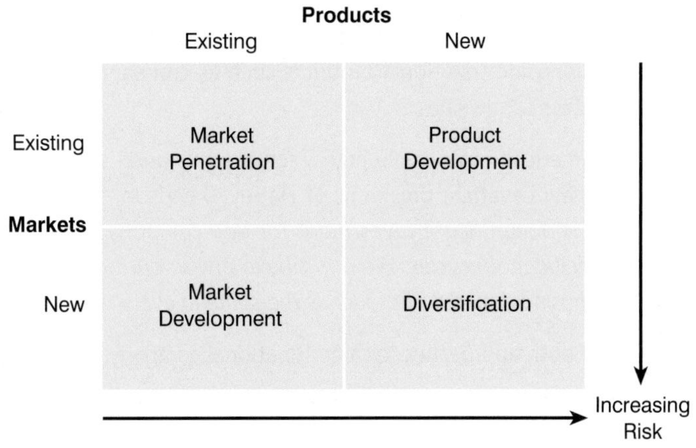

'Push' and 'pull' factors

Market penetration. The first quadrant in the Ansoff matrix represents businesses that have an existing product in an existing market. It could be said to represent those businesses that are contemplating entering an international market because of the 'push' or 'pull' factors discussed earlier (pages 33-6).

Market development is the second market growth strategy in the Ansoff matrix and is perhaps the least risky option for international expansion. This strategy is used when the business targets a new market with existing products. It is less risky because the business is using existing products of which it has experience and expertise but can be more risky because the new market has many unknowns. (Where cultural values affect customer choices, there is a danger that existing products may offend or just not sell very well.) Harley Davidson pursued such a strategy when they moved into India. Other examples include Apple and clothing firms such as Stella McCartney. These companies continue to expand their existing brands across new global markets.

Ethnocentric

Product development in the Ansoff matrix refers to businesses that have a good market share in an existing market and therefore might need to introduce new products to achieve expansion. In the international context this means businesses that have already gone through market development and are now looking to expand in the new markets by developing different products. Examples would include McDonald's, or Starbucks which have developed more local products alongside their existing ones, once they have moved in.

Diversification in the Ansoff matrix applies when the product is completely new and is being introduced into a new market. Samsung began as a trading company, later expanding into insurance, securities, food processing and retail. Today, it is a global brand mostly known for its televisions, phones and other electronic devices. However, it also has a wide range of diversified global businesses, selling semi-conductors, appliances, cameras, watches, clothing, music services, cloud computing, and home automation. It is also the world's second largest shipbuilder. Tata, the Indian multinational conglomerate is a similar example. This is considered the riskiest option because both the product and market are new and unknown.

Conglomerates

Show your understanding

1. Using the case studies in this chapter, work out where KitKat, Coca-Cola and Disney stand within Ansoff's matrix, explaining your conclusions in each case.

2. Unilever's Shakti Programme was based on the distribution of very small packages of hygiene and personal care products. These were priced to be within the reach of the target market, where incomes are growing from a very low base. Explain how Ansoff's matrix may have helped Unilever to come up with this innovative strategy.

Exam style question

Starbucks in China is easily recognisable, with its classic décor and logos. Nevertheless, it has incorporated certain aspects of Chinese art, culture and geography into the design of its stores. Local products include moon cakes during the Chinese Mid-Autumn Festival, iced rice dumplings during the Dragon Boat Festival, and Red Bean and Black Sesame Green Tea Frappuccinos year-round. These are sold alongside traditional products such as croissants, Danish pastries, sausage rolls, and turkey and cheese sandwiches.

Harley Davidson, the American motorcycle manufacturer, has been successfully selling bikes in India since 2009. Matthew Levatich, president of Harley-Davidson, spoke about their strategy. *"Product development is a significant investment for any company and our strategy is not to develop any market-specific motorcycles. We don't have any in our portfolio today and we don't have any plans to. Our business model approach is the same in every market we are in."*

Evaluate the benefits of both approaches for a multinational company. *(20 marks)*

Chapter 12

Niche markets

Terms to revise: niche markets (Theme 1).

Philatelists
The buying and selling of stamps is a global business. Embassy Philatelists got started in a very small way. Barry Fitzgerald realised he could make a living out of stamps while he was still at school. He buys, sells and auctions stamps from all over the world. The big breakthrough came with the arrival of eBay, which made it possible for many more enthusiasts to keep in touch with each other and enjoy their collecting hobby. Trading stamps is global in scope.

Organic food
Organic cheeses produced in the UK sell well over much of Europe and North America. Polish farmers export organic vegetables to the UK.

Discussion points
How are prices determined in global niche markets? Are sellers likely to face strong competition? Could organic farming be more profitable than food production generally? What difference has it made to trading philatelists to be able to access global markets?

A market niche is a smaller, more specialised segment of a larger market. For example, cars and clothing are both large markets, while hand-built sports cars and maternity wear are both niche products within those markets. In niche marketing a company focuses on a particular niche instead of an entire market.

Specialised products

There are many benefits to niche marketing. Focusing on a smaller segment of the market, a business has the ability to provide specialised services and products which will be valuable to the niche buyer. Consumer demand is likely to be more price inelastic, which may allow the seller to charge a higher price. Direct competition may be reduced. Smaller markets also allow sellers to get to know their customers better and, as a result, develop effective marketing and sales strategies. This means the company is better able to satisfy the customer; in turn, this will lead to customer loyalty and repeat sales.

Global market niches

A **global market niche** has very similar characteristics to local niche markets but operates on a global scale. Some global niches are large simply because they are global. Others are very specialised and small. For some businesses, production on a global scale is the only option as there is not enough demand in the domestic market to make the business profitable. For others, specialising in niche markets is a way to escape the increasingly tough competition from low cost foreign producers. By concentrating on a section of the market that has particular preferences and adapting their product accordingly they can differentiate and escape direct competition.

Differentiation

> **Global market niches** are smaller, more specialised parts of a global market where customers in more than one country have particular needs that are not fully met by the global mass market. The niche product or service will often be be carefully differentiated from that of the mass market.

How cultural diversity creates niche markets

Groups of people across the globe have different interests and values; niche markets are created by these divisions. For example, within the overall shoe market there is a niche market for vegans who will not buy anything made from, or involving the use of, animal products. Beyond Skin is a UK business that makes shoes using eco-friendly fabrics rather than leather.

Different cultures have different preferences based on societal or religious factors. For example, halal cosmetics are products free from materials forbidden by Islamic Law – usually made entirely from natural plant-based ingredients, with no animal or alcohol ingredients used. The halal cosmetics market in Saudi Arabia is projected to grow over 15% between 2015 and 2020 and is expected to expand into western economies as well.

Vegans who buy non-leather shoes or women who buy halal cosmetics are found all over the world and from many different nationalities but they all share the same underlying reason for becoming customers of that particular global niche market. They have shared values that create a **subculture** that spans continents. This idea applies to many different products and services from diverse fields such as fashion, culture and leisure. Many manufacturers know this and exploit these global market niches to gain a competitive advantage.

> **Subcultures** are groups of people who have interests and values in common. They may be based on hobbies, life-styles, ethnic or religious background or just personal enthusiasms and preferences. People who belong to subcultures do not necessarily communicate with each other but the internet makes it easy to keep in touch.

Brand loyalty

Gatorade makes a beverage that contains electrolytes and minerals used before, after and during physical activity. It is aimed at athletes. A marketing analyst set out to examine brand perceptions about Gatorade. The results showed that the subgroup of consumers who regarded themselves as 'real athletes' had a much stronger perception of the brand value of Gatorade, and therefore loyalty to it, than 'non-athletes'. This enabled Gatorade to target the athletes much more precisely and effectively with other products related to Gatorade.

> **Think!**
> Identify a niche product that you have at some time bought, or at least considered. Was your choice cultural or based on a hobby? Analyse your reasons for buying it.

Niche products and the digital economy

Internet advertising

A small business that is in close contact with its market through internet advertising may look for ways to add value to its products in the way that Gatorade did. This helps the business to achieve a high degree of market penetration. People in niche markets are quite likely to know each other and to pass on information about products that have been designed to fulfil their needs. There is a connection here to the idea of the 'Long Tail', which refers to the large number of products that have very small markets. This was spelt out in 'The Long Tail: Why the Future of Business is Selling Less of More' by Chris Anderson.

Figure 1: The Long Tail

The Long Tail

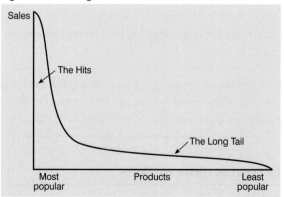

In Figure 1 you can see that sales of 'the hits' are very high and correspond to the mass produced items that very many people buy. Obviously these are associated with widespread advertising and large markets that include all sorts of different people. There may be differentiated rival products, but these relate to

Accessible markets

general fitness for purpose rather than very personal preferences – as with, say, toothpaste or vacuum cleaners. The long tail shows the very large number of specialised niche products aimed at small markets and designed to meet very specific needs and preferences. There may be shops here and there that sell products located in the long tail, but very often the business will be mainly digital.

The diagram illustrates the way many niche products can actually be profitable if they are tailored to a known and probably also a digitally accessible market. Tiny companies can survive by having customers who are widely spread out but together, add up to a viable market. They do not need to depend on a domestic market that is too small to be profitable.

> **Wardell Armstrong**
>
> Wardell Armstrong Mining and Quarrying have been providing expert advice to the UK mining industry for over 170 years. In recent decades their mining services have expanded globally to cover specialised aspects of mineral resource exploration and extraction. They now employ 480 people.
>
> Projects include exploration and resource assessment of mineral reserves all over the world. They have offices in the UK, Kazakhstan and China. Recent projects have seen them at work in Mongolia, Russia, Peru and the Arctic.
>
> Their specialised service means that they operate in a global market providing guidance and assistance to many different organisations, businesses and governments who lack their experience and in-depth skills.
>
> Wardell Armstrong also has other niche interests: it offers consultancy services for a range of environmental and archaeological projects and it has a separate legal department. All work well because their market is global in scope.
>
> 1. In what ways does Wardell Armstrong benefit from having a global market?
>
> 2. Are there any drawbacks to running a medium-sized business with global reach?

Features of global niche markets

Global niche marketing is usually to do with marketing a differentiated or specialist product to one or more very small market segments. Many businesses operating in global niches are classed as small to medium size enterprises (SMEs). The EU defines these as businesses employing less than 250 staff. In fact some 99% of all businesses in Europe are classed in this manner, accounting for around 50% of all employment.

Market orientation

These global niches can be found in both mature and expanding markets. They do not include small firms selling undifferentiated products in a global market. Rather, they offer a product or service that is distinctive and clearly recognised as such by potential customers. Features of successful global niche businesses will include:

● Clear understanding of the needs of their customers and their chosen market.

● High levels of customer service.

● Expertise in their field.

● Prioritising profit rather than market share.

● Innovation to satisfy changes in market requirements.

● Focus on cost efficiency but not at the expense of quality.

● Using the marketing mix as appropriate for the differing niches.

Application and adaptation of the marketing mix (4Ps) to suit global niches

Global niche markets require a marketing mix that is adapted to the international framework so as to gain the maximum benefit for the business. Market orientation is vital to success.

Knowing PED (roughly) matters

Price is perhaps the most obvious factor because niche markets usually have less fierce competition than mass markets; in fact they may have very little or none at all. If there are direct rivals, then they are likely to be clearly differentiated in terms of branding and image, thus reducing the impact of competition. In effect, the number of substitutes is limited and the price elasticity of demand is likely to be low. This means that price becomes less of an issue and most niche markets are able to charge higher or premium prices and maintain higher profit margins. In some niche markets high prices signify the exclusiveness and desirability of the product. Businesses do need to understand customer needs in specific markets.

Show your understanding

L'Occitane charges high prices for various fragrant skin-care products that are very appealing to many people. Probably relatively few people buy them for themselves; much more likely, the buyers are looking for gifts that are of high quality but not so expensive that they are unaffordable. Competing products are generally sold in department stores and airports. L'Occitane widened their appeal by selling through carefully designed shops that are attractive just to be in and also by stressing their Mediterranean roots.

1. L'Occitane's market is quite large, as well as global. Can it really be described as a niche market? Explain your answer.

2. Does L'Occitane have direct competitors? Identify those you can think of and explain how they are differentiated.

3. Explain L'Occitane's pricing policy.

Distinctive products

The **Product** can appear on the surface to be similar to mass market products such as the vegan shoe. Alternatively it may be highly specialised and technical, such as tunnel boring machines, or it can be unique, such as hand-made jewellery. The important factor is that something distinguishes the product and sets it apart from the mass market. It may even be the case that there is no difference but if potential customers perceive it to be different it still matters. A designer t-shirt is still just a t-shirt but the logo or label or design adds value.

Promotion is also likely to be different. By their nature, global niche markets are limited in size and customers are spread over large areas. TV advertising or sponsorship of mass events is likely to be too

L'Occitane charges high prices for various fragrant skin-care products that are very appealing to many people.

On-line communication

expensive, so advertising and promotion is targeted through specialist magazines or websites that are more likely to be seen by a significant proportion of the target market. Sometimes little promotion is necessary; with the internet and efficient search engines, potential customers can easily find and contact a niche business.

Place also benefits from modern communications and the internet. Niche producers are no longer confined to one geographical region but can operate all over the world. With modern distribution systems and increasing numbers of global consumers having access to the internet, and becoming more willing to use it for commercial purposes, the global niche producer has been able to overcome many of the physical restrictions of the past.

Think!

Describe a business in a global niche market that you know. Show how its marketing policy illustrates the use of conventional marketing strategies in a way that suits its global market. Draw on your work on previous chapters to help you to do this.

American University in Cairo Press (AUC)

Established in 1960 the AUC Press has become the Middle East's leading English-language publishing house. Its goals and purposes reflect and support the mission of its parent university in education, research, and cultural exchange through professional publishing and bookselling services. It is particularly well-known for its publications on Archaeology, History, Literature and Islamic Studies.

Its rapidly expanding publishing program of high quality scholarly and general interest publications on Egypt and the Middle East currently offers up to 80 new books annually. It maintains a backlist of some 800 titles for distribution worldwide. Through its bookstores and distributors in Egypt and abroad, the AUC Press sells more than 300,000 books every year. It licenses foreign editions of Naguib Mahfouz (Nobel prize winner for literature) and other Arab writers in 40 languages.

1. What evidence can you find to suggest that the AUC Press operates in a global niche market?

2. What kinds of marketing issues might the AUC Press encounter and how would it address these?

3. How might AUC Press decide on a pricing policy?

Cultural divergence

In the 1990s Walmart wanted to set up retail outlets in Germany. Already, Walmart was the world's biggest retailer, with 3,800 supermarkets in the USA alone. It found a chain that looked promising and immediately turned all the outlets into American-style stores. It didn't work. German employees felt alienated by the requirements of the 'have a nice day' style and the shoppers didn't like it either. It all felt fake to them. Walmart put an American in charge of the operation; he didn't speak German and wanted everyone to speak English. After a few years of losses, Walmart gave up and sold the chain to one of its competitors, Metro.

Discussion points

What ought Walmart to have done before making the move into Germany? You should have at least five suggestions. Justify your recommendations.

This chapter explores many aspects of business expansion in international markets. Most of the references to cultural differences apply equally to businesses that are looking for offshoring opportunities and businesses that are looking for new markets.

Cultural differences

Social and cultural differences can be very significant. They have to be taken into account in any activity that involves collaboration between different groups of people. Their impact is easily underestimated. From inside our own culture, we might imagine that all human beings have similar aspirations and expectations. We would be quite wrong.

Shared values

The term 'culture' refers to the shared attitudes, values, customs and expectations that define groups of people. Social differences come into play when different groups of people have different ways of communicating and different expectations about the way people customarily behave. Values are the principles that guide people in their relations with each other. We can talk about cultural differences between societies, nations or economies. But we might also talk about differences between groups that can be identified within individual nation states. These are often the basis for market segments.

> **Social and cultural differences** come from the fact that individual societies and groups within them may have a distinctive way of life. This will affect their patterns of consumption and the products they favour. But it will also affect the way they do business with one another.

Corporate cultures

Different businesses have different corporate cultures. These are the assumptions that are shared by people working together; they influence the ways in which decisions are taken. They may include an expectation that people will be flexible. But sometimes people are very inflexible, taking decisions about product design and marketing that suit their own existing objectives. If firms with inflexible business models start to expand abroad, they can encounter difficulties. Unfamiliar national and local cultures can confound their expectations about the markets in which they propose to operate. They may also find that the people with whom they want to do business have unfamiliar

Unfamiliar cultures

Social and cultural differences have to be taken into account in any activity that involves collaboration between different groups of people.

habits and conventions. If they are to communicate effectively with potential partners, they will have to respect local patterns of behaviour.

All businesses that are looking to operate in unfamiliar markets will encounter cultural differences in their initial contacts with business people in the location they are exploring. It helps to know how people do business there.

In Asia, it is useful to know:

Learning local conventions

- Holding a business card with both hands when presenting it is a simple way to observe the Asian custom.

- It is wise to avoid talking about sensitive political issues because being criticised or losing face is always very problematic for people from the Far East, especially China and Japan. But criticism is seldom appreciated anywhere.

In general, businesses need to allow plenty of time for getting to know new markets, planning their strategies and recruiting knowledgeable local managers. Businesses that are offshoring to cut production costs do not need to worry about market research and product design but they do need to be sure that their suppliers understand what they need and know how to deliver it.

Different tastes

Appropriate design

The basic rule here is never simply to assume that if customers in one country like the product, customers in other countries will too. Product design can be crucial in determining sales levels. Detailed knowledge of the market in question is needed to ensure that designs are appropriate. This applies to services (as with Walmart) as well as goods.

Example

The Marriott International hotel chain took local differences into account in the design of its various websites. In Japan they found that Japanese customers preferred to click on a series of small maps rather than type in an address or area code. This adaptation increased site performance by 19% in the first two weeks alone.

For Arab countries, they use photos of landscapes, nature, or buildings for their websites. The photos rarely include people so as not to show objectionable attire to the local audience.

In China the site features a blue field to reflect local preferences for style and the local association of the colour blue with luxury.

Tastes, fashions and preferences vary considerably from one market to another. Market research is essential to ensure that:

Customer preferences

- the nature of the product fits consumer requirements.
- the price is appropriate for the target market.
- promotional activity communicates in ways that people will find meaningful.
- distribution arrangements are consistent with consumer expectations.

Example

Deloitte's research shows that 40% of businesses that compete in emerging markets now get their products designed locally. Unilever, the giant manufacturer of food and household products, has set up 68 different innovation centres across 20 countries. They study local markets and devise the products that best meet their needs. Unilever's approach means that they can cater for different market segments or regions within countries.

Studying local markets

Businesses that want to expand into new markets must allow time to get to know their target markets. They must seek out partners and decide whether a joint venture may be appropriate (pages 52-3). They will need to find local agents and perhaps also hire local employees who have a good understanding of the

Market research

relevant markets. They may decide to trial some products in a small area. All of these preparations require up-front investment – and that is just to get the necessary market research in place. Only after that can the planning process move on to product design, production and marketing.

A big mistake at Whirlpool

Whirlpool, the white goods manufacturer, wanted to produce a 'World Washer'. It would be a single, standardised model, designed to suit a wide range of markets and simple enough to be priced competitively and sell to people on middle incomes in emerging economies. It was launched in Brazil, Mexico, China and India. The machine sold well – except in India. Whirlpool had invested heavily in distribution systems, designed to reach a potentially huge but geographically fragmented market. It sent a team to India to find out what had gone wrong.

The team discovered that many traditional Indian garments are made from fine silk or cotton. They were getting caught in a one millimeter gap around the edge of the drum. Whirlpool redesigned the machine to suit the Indian market. Eventually it recouped its losses but that took many years.

Whirlpool had assumed that all its target markets were much the same. The designers of the World Washer did not know about clothing styles in India.

Questions

1. Why do many firms make mistakes when they look to sell their products in new markets?

2. Suggest two ways in which Whirlpool might have avoided this mistake and explain how they might have worked.

Language

Communication

The way people communicate can vary hugely from one economy to another. Obviously language barriers operate at every level. Businesses need bilingual people who can advise them on how to avoid the pitfalls. But there are many other sources of difficulty.

● Conventions in business discussions differ greatly; potential business partners have to be approached in ways that will not offend them. This means that people who are going to negotiate deals in culturally different economies have to be very well briefed so as to avoid possible misunderstandings.

Avoiding misunderstandings

● Differences in the way people communicate must also be explored before planning advertising campaigns and promotional activities.

● Gestures that are friendly in one culture may be anything but, in another. In the matter of building trust, quite small misunderstandings can prove to be setbacks.

● The key requirement is to spend time finding out how to behave, without offending potential allies, in the context of the relevant national culture. Body language can be just as, if not more, important than speech. It makes sense not to speak for too long if using an interpreter.

Meaningful marketing

● The marketing message itself will have to be set out in terms that are meaningful and appropriate to the culture in question. Literal translations of advertising slogans are particularly likely to fail. Brand names may need to be adapted.

● All this confirms that preparing to enter a new market is usually more costly than exporters expect.

Knowing how to behave

Examples

Most Asians expect to spend a long time chatting about apparently irrelevant matters before serious negotiation begins. This is particularly true in China and Japan. Whatever the size of the project, time spent at the start, including eating meals together, is definitely not wasted. This gives everyone a chance to learn about each other and establish a degree of trust.

In many parts of Africa, a limp handshake is appropriate. Furthermore, a handshake in Africa may well last several minutes, while in the USA a handshake that is even a few seconds too long seems like excessive familiarity.

Unintended meanings and inappropriate or inaccurate translations

Past mistakes

When Pepsi first started to sell in the Chinese market, they used the slogan that was current at the time, 'Pepsi Brings you Back to Life'. The drink didn't sell well. Translated directly into Chinese, the slogan meant, 'Pepsi Brings Your Ancestors Back from the Grave'. Swift changes were made but such gaffes can be damaging for quite a while.

Translating business and marketing messages into another language can be fraught with difficulties and this is where the use of native speakers is imperative. The internet is full of such examples, many of which are genuine and some apocryphal. Here are some more examples.

- Braniff International Airlines translated a slogan touting its finely upholstered seats 'Fly in Leather' into Spanish as 'Fly Naked'.
- Clairol launched a hair-curling iron called 'Mist Stick' in Germany even though 'mist' is German slang for manure.
- Coca-Cola's brand name, when first marketed in China, was sometimes translated as 'Bite The Wax Tadpole'.
- Coors breweries translated its slogan, 'Turn It Loose', into Spanish, where it is a colloquial term for having diarrhoea.

Many of these mistakes go back to the early days of globalisation. Few businesses nowadays would fail to check the local meanings of their promotions. But the mistakes illustrate the importance of careful preparation when moving into new markets.

Avoiding inappropriate branding and promotion

Culture and brand image

There is a more serious side to cultural awareness. Inappropriate branding and promotion can cause great offence and result in real damage to sales and reputation. There are some obvious areas to avoid, particularly where religious beliefs are a significant element in the local culture.

Brands often help to create customer confidence in new markets. They also make it easy for people to pass on their satisfaction in a new purchase to friends and family. So they have clear promotional value but of course, this only works if the brand image is appropriate to the local culture. There are no short cuts to this kind of success. But if a whole range of business activities are employed to prepare the way for breaking into the new market, success may be achieved.

Recipes for success

Learning to communicate	Doing market research	Starting up in business
Clarifying language and meanings; using interpreters effectively.	Investigating local preferences and expectations.	Differentiating products to make them appropriate to the relevant market.
Developing awareness of appropriate gestures and body language.	Understanding cultural divergences – knowing what is acceptable.	Using market strategies that fit the local situation and conform to expecations.
Adopting local business conventions.	Identifying potential market segments.	
Working with joint ventures.		Working with local people who can advise and be part of the development team.
Taking time to develop trust.	Working out possible pricing strategies that match consumer demand.	

Many MNCs are now well aware of the need for careful preparation. Unilever has a culture of its own that is sharply focused on the study of local markets. Many of its products are culturally sensitive; it could not survive without its tradition of studying the needs of different customer groups. Whirlpool's mistake was in the design of the product rather than its promotion. But once discovered, the problem was rectified, despite the great expense. Businesses that experience a situation like the Walmart venture into Germany may be making a good decision when they withdraw from the market.

The most successful businesses can adapt to change by keeping themselves well informed and moving swiftly when the facts change.

Reducing risk

Many businesses have made serious money by breaking into new markets. But many have found their new markets extremely risky. Some have withdrawn while others continue to pour money into their projects in the hope of long term gains. Potential rewards are often high but risks are very significant.

Being well informed about cultural differences can reduce the risks. The most successful businesses are nimble – they can adapt to change by keeping themselves well informed and moving swiftly when the facts change. They are flexible enough to work within differing cultures and take complex decisions on the basis of accurate information. This requires willingness to invest time and money in the planning process.

Find out

Many British retailers have tried to break into new foreign markets. Some have done well – Tesco's big successes are in Poland and S. Korea. But many (including Tesco in other countries) have faced poor profits. Some have simply closed down and written off the expenses, while others have struggled on. Some commentators say the basic problem was that UK managers always thought they knew everything they needed to know... Find out which retailers have recently set up new outlets abroad and see how they are performing. It appears that many think they have now learnt from the mistakes of others.

Exam style question

Evaluate the extent to which cultural differences create difficulties for businesses that want to start multinational projects.

(20 marks)

Chapter 14

The impact of MNCs

Terms to revise: corporate social responsibility (CSR, Theme 3), FDI (Chapters 2-3),

India and MNCs

Between 1991 and 2012, the number of MNCs in India more than quadrupled. And over 20 years, total MNC revenue grew at a compound annual rate of 18% – much faster than the overall economy.

By 2014, the top two MNCs in India were Maruti Suzuki and Samsung Electronics, each accounting for just around 5% of total MNC revenue. Between October 2014 and April 2015 India received $19.84bn in FDI compared to $13.4bn for the same period in the previous year, an increase of 48%.

Discussion points

What impact might the rapid increase in the number of MNCs have on the Indian economy?

Identify possible problems that might arise from the changes.

MNCs were first looked at in Chapters 2 and 3; this section looks in more detail at the impact they have on local and national economies. Some, by their sheer size, have a global impact. For example Walmart operates in 28 countries and has a turnover greater than Poland's GDP. Many have considerable market power.

Comparing MNC revenue with GDP data

Table 1: Turnover of the 5 largest MNCs by comparison with 5 countries' nominal GDP (estimated 2016)

Ranking	Country / Company	GDP / Revenue ($m)
6	United Kingdom	2,760,960
1	Walmart	482,130
21	Poland	473,501
2	State Grid	329,601
32	United Arab Emirates	325,135
3	China National Petroleum	299,271
39	Singapore	294,560
4	Sinopec	294,344
5	Royal Dutch Shell	272,156
40	South Africa	266,213
41	Ireland	254,596

Source: Fortune, Global 500 and World Bank

How and why have MNCs grown in this way?

Extension strategies

● **Access to new markets**: for many MNCs, domestic markets are saturated. Future growth and rising profits must come from expansion overseas where rising incomes can be tempting. Entering new markets can act as an extension strategy for the product life cycle. But the strategy can be misused. Some big tobacco companies have increased cigarette sales in developing countries. In 2015 one of them was believed to have lobbied the Pakistani government not to require health warnings on cigarette packs. There are moves to discourage some governments from implementing the UN World Health Organisation's Framework Convention on Tobacco Control. This type of activity is unethical and can give some MNCs a very bad name.

Economies of scale reduce unit cost

- **Reducing costs**: expansion overseas can yield substantial cost savings. Economies of scale can reduce the unit costs of standardised products, enhancing competitive advantage. Unskilled labour may be cheaper, more available and less regulated. Now, many countries can offer labour that is cheap, skilled and adaptable as well. Jobs are created and incomes rise.

The global management consulting firm A.T. Kearney's Global Services Location Index (GSLI), a ranking of the most attractive offshoring destinations, placed India at the top with China and Malaysia second and third (2016). Brazil, Colombia, Romania, Chile and Latvia have all made significant gains in position. Labour is not the only cost that can be saved; proximity to markets can also be significant. Mexico is benefiting from being next-door to the world's largest economy, the USA.

- **Controlling resources**: many businesses have to follow the resources to extract and process them. Companies that rely on a secure and preferably cheap source of raw materials are likely to expand where they are found. Examples include minerals, petrochemicals and many commodities. MNCs are currently vying to gain access to Arctic and Antarctic mineral and oil reserves. They may try to secure resources for future growth by preventing rivals from acquiring them. Several MNCs would like to get access to Bolivia's lithium deposits (see the example on page 38).

- Taking advantage of governments and getting round trade barriers: many governments offer substantial incentives to attract MNCs to their countries. In 2009 Dell computers moved its manufacturing plant from County Limerick in Ireland to Lodz in Poland. A major factor in this decision was a €52.7 million aid package offered by the Polish Government.

MNC objectives

As part of its 'Make in India' campaign, the Indian government is offering subsidies and tax concessions to certain sectors, for example to boost manufacturing in the electronics sector a capital subsidy of 25% for 10 years is on offer.

Businesses that wish to penetrate markets to avoid tariffs or quotas will often move production into that area. Toyota began to produce in the USA to access NAFTA markets.

- **Travel and technologies** have improved, making it much easier to organise and co-ordinate business operations around the world. Email and video conferencing have made some travel obsolete. New trade blocs, market liberalisation and the WTO, the expansion of India, opening up in China and the fall of communism in Europe have all encouraged the spread and growth of MNCs.

Email and video conferencing have made some travel obsolete.

The impact of MNCs on local economies

Multinationals are often welcomed in overseas countries; they can bring many benefits with them. These benefits apply to a range of stakeholders including the people, the government, other businesses and the economy as a whole. Their impact will also, for some, be negative.

MNC activity cuts both ways

Examples

General Electric is developing a tele-diagnostic health service with a local start-up, SevenSeas, in Kenya. This enables remote clinics to screen local people, sending the data to be analysed in a central hub. This will provide rapid answers to help the health care workers find the right treatments.

Not all MNCs take care to ensure that their employees have satisfactory working conditions and reasonable pay. The majority of businesses that build and own production facilities in emerging economies make sure that their employees are better off with them than with a local employer. But many MNCs that outsource their production to independent local businesses do not interfere with pay or working conditions. Jobs may be created but they may involve risks that would not be acceptable in developed economies.

Local labour, wages, working conditions and job creation

Local spending

Starting operations in an overseas economy involves a flow of capital to fund the creation of productive capacity (FDI). Even if help is offered by the host government, there will still be considerable direct expenditure. Even a modest sized production plant will require land and materials for construction. Very often these resources and the labour needed to construct the plant will come from the host country. Builders, joiners, electricians and many others will be needed to complete the project. All of this will create local employment and income.

Once the plant opens it may employ many local people – depending upon the skills needed and the skills available. Often managers from the parent country will run the operation and employ and train local people. Once production starts the plant will create more employment for other businesses.

Weak regulation

Most MNCs say that they conform to the laws of the country they are operating in. However, outside the developed economies, employment law is relatively lax and health and safety regulations are much less stringent. Weak regulation is one of the ways in which labour costs are kept low in developing and emerging economies.

Local businesses

Indirect benefits

Supplies and services will be needed by the incoming MNC and this is an opportunity for local firms to start up or expand existing operations. An MNC may need raw materials, components, transport, maintenance services, cleaners, packaging materials and so on. This creates employment and income, some of which will be spent in local shops and businesses, increasing demand for other goods and services, creating more employment. In other words a positive regional multiplier effect occurs. Indirect job creation is estimated by the UN to be three times the number directly generated by MNCs in manufacturing. It is seven times the number in food processing.

> **Show your understanding**
>
> PepsiCo Ireland first came to Cork in 1974, producing concentrate for well established brands such as Pepsi, Diet Pepsi, 7Up, Mountain Dew, Sierra Mist, Mirinda and Gatorade at a plant at Little Island. In 2003 PepsiCo invested over $100 million in a state-of-the-art second manufacturing facility at a greenfield site in Carrigaline. In 2006 a satellite R&D centre was also established at Little Island.
>
> In 2007 PepsiCo transferred its Worldwide Concentrate headquarters from New York to Cork. A third location was established at Eastgate which oversees PepsiCo's entire global concentrate operations and a new pilot R&D plant was also established.
>
> PepsiCo Ireland now employs over 500 people at its three locations in Cork. The business activities located in Cork include the manufacture of concentrate (exported to 105 countries worldwide), laboratories, financial shared services (supporting 65 countries), IT providing support to global operations, R&D, Global Market Intelligence and concentrate functions.
>
> 1. Suggest reasons why PepsiCo chose Cork as a location.
>
> 2. Analyse the impact PepsiCo may have had on Ireland's economy.
>
> 3. Assess the impact PepsiCo may have had on local people and local businesses.

Local businesses may find it hard to compete

Subsidies

Sometimes multinationals may have a negative impact on local businesses. If they receive favourable treatment from the host governments, such as tax breaks or other forms of financial assistance, they are effectively being subsidised. Local firms may become less competitive, lose market share and see a fall in profitability. It is often the case that the newer and usually more efficient MNC operations require less labour than the local businesses that close. Even without subsidies they may be in direct competition with local businesses that are not as efficient as the MNC. This can cause the local businesses to lose customers and even fail. This is one of the accusations levelled against the fast food chains in places like India as they take custom away from long established local restaurants.

Competition may hurt

When Shell (Anglo-Dutch), Chevron (US) and Texaco (US) started operating in Nigeria, the Nigerian National Petroleum Corporation (NNPC) suffered as a result and lost their prominent market position. In 2009 Walmart opened a wholesale store in India. For a while India's strict commercial laws prevented much in the way of expansion or direct competition but in 2016 the laws were relaxed. There is widespread concern amongst India's countless small retailers that many of them will lose their livelihoods. Toyota's move to manufacture in the USA undoubtedly did much to hasten the demise of the American motor industry. Fifty years ago, American car companies dominated the world, especially General Motors, many of whose factories were based in Flint, Michigan, 40 miles north of Detroit. Today there are only 6,000 GM workers in Flint, compared to 100,000 at its peak, and the town and workers are suffering.

The local community and environment

Many multinationals have CSR and ethical policies that they try to adhere to. To the extent that they succeed, they will often prove to be the kind of employers that many people really want to work for. If MNCs take care to offer better pay than local employers, they will usually be looked on favourably.

Helping communities

Some companies go beyond simply improving on local wage rates. They try to help the local economy to develop. Others want to help by devising products that will address the greatest needs of poorer people in the communities where they operate. Bernard Giraud, Director of Sustainable Development and Social Responsibility at Groupe Danone, said *"Selling to the poor is not sustainable business. It is not simply about affordability… the products and services provided must bring clear social value to the impoverished."*

Grameen Danone Foods ltd.

A joint venture was started in Bangladesh by Danone and the Grameen Bank (the 'Bank of the poor') in March 2006. They launched a yoghurt called Shokti Doi, designed to meet the nutritional needs of Bangladeshi children and improve their health. It is made from local cow's milk and date molasses and sells for just 5p.

The whole of the production and distribution system has been constructed with the aim of creating as many jobs as possible within the local community. Local farmers provide the raw materials and also benefit from micro-credits offered by the Grameen Bank to start up or expand their businesses. Danone provides technical expertise. The pots are entirely biodegradable. Shokti Doi is distributed using a system based on the so-called 'Grameen Ladies' who make sales door-to-door. They receive a small commission on each pot sold.

This activity should provide income to more than 1,600 persons within a radius of 30 km around each plant. Some 600,000 are sold each week. There are plans to have 50 mini plants in operation by 2020, to meet the needs of 150 million people.

Think!

In what different ways can CSR contribute to alleviating poverty in the least developed economies?

Grameen Danone is a social business. Besides Danone, there are other companies that are committed to helping maintain or improve the local conditions and the environment.

Impact of MNCs on national economies

Tax revenue

MNCs should have a wider beneficial impact on the economy of the host nation whether it is a sophisticated developed economy such as the UK or a developing economy such as Vietnam. Increases in employment and wage levels should generate a larger taxpayer base, providing the government with increased revenue. Profits from MNCs can be taxed, again adding to revenues which can be used to fund further development. At the same time there may be a reduction in government expenditure if some form of benefits had previously been paid to the unemployed. Higher incomes should help many local businesses.

MNCs and corporate tax rates

The number of multinational companies wanting to move to Britain jumped by 50% in 2013. By the end of 2014, more than 60 firms were looking at relocating their global or regional headquarters to Britain in the near future. A report by the accountancy firm Ernst & Young suggested that the influx of multinationals to Britain was due to government policies, including lower corporation tax.

In 2010, UK corporation tax was 28%. That year, Chancellor George Osborne cut the rate to 24%. He later made further cuts so that by 2016 it was 20%. He said: *"This is very welcome news and it shows our economic plan is working. Global companies used to move away from the UK. Thanks to our reforms to the tax system and our clear signals to the world that Britain is open for business, they are coming back."*

1. Explain two reasons why George Osborne cut the rate of corporation tax in the
   UK during his term of office.   *(8 marks)*

2. Assess the impact this could have on the UK economy.   *(12 marks)*

Business taxes

FDI flows

Most economies are likely to benefit from FDI flows in many different ways; this is why the UK Chancellor was so keen to cut corporation tax in 2010-13. The advantages that MNC investment brings to host countries can be considerable. Both MNC involvement and FDI can be major drivers of growth and a route out of poverty. China is a good example of this; FDI in the year to November 2009 rose by 32%, as the country's rapid recovery from the global economic downturn attracted more overseas money. Although it has slowed down since then it is still significant. (See Table 3, page 19 for useful data.)

It is not just the poorer nations that gain. Much FDI still finds its way to the richer economies. The $3.1 trillion stock of FDI in the United States at the end of 2016 (accumulated over many years) is the equivalent of approximately 18% of US gross domestic product (GDP).

Figure 1: FDI inflows, US$ billions

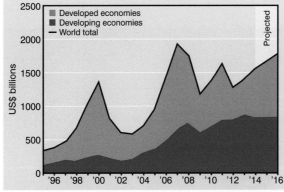

Source: UNCTAD (United Nations Conference on Trade and Development).
N.B. Most emerging economies are included in the developing countries group.
The projected growth for developed economies in 2014-16 may be rather optimistic.

FDI in developing economies

FDI flows into developing economies have steadily increased, particularly since the early 2000s. The total fluctuates year by year, particularly for the developed economies, due to uncertainties in the wider economic environment. The impact of the financial crisis in 2008 can clearly be seen here. Despite these variations the overall trend is a long-term increase and a quadrupling between 1995 and 2016.

Find out
Research FDI flows to find out which countries receive the most FDI and which flows are increasing the most rapidly.

Balance of payments

Current account

The balance of payments (BoP) is the difference in total value between payments into and out of a country over a period of time. It is a record of all financial transactions between consumers, businesses and governments of one country with the rest of the world. The BoP shows how much money comes into a country compared with how much goes out. The current account measures the amount of goods and services imported and exported. The capital account measures flows of capital.

> The **balance of payments** is a record of all transactions associated with imports and exports, and all international capital movements.

A trade deficit

Ideally the BoP should be a positive figure. In 2015 the UK BoP had a deficit of £96.2bn which means that £96.2bn more money left the UK than entered it. A deficit needs to be financed and one of the government's main macroeconomic objectives is to keep it as low as possible. A deficit can be cleared if the exchange rate depreciates. This increases competitiveness, making it easy to sell more exports. But it also raises the cost of imports.

Capital inflows

FDI inflows help with this, which is another reason why governments are keen to attract them. When an MNC arrives it invests capital to create production facilities, an inflow of money. It then produces and exports goods or services that create another inflow of money from foreign buyers. Exporting cars made in the UK by Honda, Toyota and Nissan has a positive impact on the UK BoP. At the same time UK consumers may buy goods produced by MNCs in the UK, which reduces the level of imports.

On the other hand the MNCs may import raw materials and components. People who are employed by the MNCs may spend more of their income on foreign goods. Both actions increase imports and increase the BoP deficit.

Technology and skills transfer

Technology transfer

FDI from an MNC brings with it a set of skills and technologies, of which the host country may have little or no experience. Although the skills and technology are used by the MNC for its own benefit, some of them will 'rub-off' or transfer to the host country. The degree to which this happens depends on the nature of the business and the complexity of the process.

The balance of payments is the difference in total value between payments into and out of a country over a period of time.

> **Technology transfer** occurs when countries acquire techniques they did not have through contacts with other countries that are technically more advanced.

MNCs may teach new skills

When a new business opens, some of the jobs it offers may require training which the MNC can provide. As the local workers are trained they become more skilled and this increasing skill level can benefit the local and national economy. MNCs often teach local workers the skills needed to operate sophisticated production systems. This training is transferred when employees change jobs. Locals trained as managers gain insights into business activities that might otherwise not be available to them. By developing closer links with domestic suppliers, MNCs, through their subsidiaries, can transfer valuable techniques to domestic businesses.

Technologies, knowledge and skills are transferred to local economies through supply linkages, competition, and labour turnover. Newly developed systems become available when they are imported by MNCs. Experience of new production and engineering techniques, which may not otherwise be available to local enterprises, can be a catalyst for innovation among local entrepreneurs.

Learning new techniques

Many MNCs have found, to their dismay, that industrial espionage and copycat production can be a hazard when locating abroad. Copyright and intellectual property rights (IPR) can be difficult to protect. In the past, China was notorious in this respect, but the problem has diminished considerably. Subcontracting arrangements introduce new technologies to local businesses, giving them the opportunity to enhance or adapt new techniques for the domestic market.

The benefit to the host country of technology transfer is particularly important for its export industries. Advanced equipment reduces production costs; combined with relatively inexpensive labour, it may lead to lower prices and increased volume, making the host country more competitive. Export promotion is an important part of many countries' growth strategies. The Chinese appliance maker Haier (see below) has undoubtedly benefited from flows of FDI which have changed work practices and standards there. Along with many other firms it is now exporting its goods to the developed countries. Much of the growth in the economies of Taiwan, Hong Kong and South Korea is due to technology transfer including technical know-how, managerial skills and marketing techniques.

Learning managerial skills

Haier

In the 1920s a refrigerator factory was built in Quingdao to supply the Chinese market. After the 1949 communist revolution, Haier was taken over and turned into a state owned enterprise (SOE).

By the 1980s the factory had debts of over ¥1.4 million and suffered from dilapidated infrastructure, poor management, and lack of quality controls, resulting from the centrally planned system. Production had slowed down to such an extent that production rarely passed 80 refrigerators a month; the factory was close to bankruptcy. Salvation came in the form of a new young manager, Zhang Ruimin who was appointed as managing director in 1984.

Zhang decided to use Western and Japanese business practices and management techniques. When he arrived, he realised that the poor condition of the factory's quality controls was endangering its continued survival. Zhang achieved the transformation through a joint venture with a German appliance maker, Liebherr. They transferred the technology and know-how to manufacture household appliances.

The factory began its recovery by licensing refrigerator technology from Liebherr. The installation of Liebherr's equipment and technology was accompanied by a new and rigorous commitment to quality. Haier adopted its name from the 'herr' in the German company's name.

"The first year, we had 600 employees and 300,000 yuan ($35,000) in sales. We were bankrupt," Zhang said. Since then, Haier has become the world's largest manufacturer of white goods and has diversified into phones and laptop computers.

In January, 2016 Haier Group acquired General Electric's appliance division for $5.4bn.

Question

Evaluate the role and significance of technology transfer in the development of the Haier Group.

Consumers

Rising living standards

As a consumer in a developed country, you are surrounded by MNCs' products. They have a considerable impact on your lifestyle. Without imports, people in the UK would have very restricted choices and some products would not be available. In their drive for success and profit, MNCs compete to provide consumers with increased choice and often lower prices. Rising incomes have created new markets. FDI can affect the lives of consumers in other ways too. New infrastructure can improve transport and communications. Multinational pharmaceutical companies can develop new drugs and treatments.

Competition keeps prices down

Up to a point, people in emerging economies benefit from these developments too. The key factor is competition. Globalisation creates more competitive markets but sometimes, the MNCs concerned become so powerful that these benefits are threatened. We rely on competition law to prevent companies from charging prices that are way above production costs.

> **Think!**
> Which markets are most likely to become more competitive as globalisation develops?

Downsides for consumers may include pollution and environmental degradation, poor working conditions for some and products that cause harm to society, such as tobacco. The obesity crisis is often blamed on many food and fast food producers, most of whom are MNCs.

MNCs are often blamed for their role in the erosion of local and traditional ways of life. Their products swamp and replace products from the local culture. It is not just the products themselves; critics argue that this also brings in mainly western ideas and, in particular, American ones. The imposition of this alien corporate culture is seen as a retrograde step.

Local cultures and businesses may suffer

With branches in over 120 countries and 47 million customers a day, the golden arches of McDonald's are now, according to Eric Schlosser's Fast Food Nation, "more widely recognised than the Christian cross." McDonald's may be an easy target but the same idea applies to drinks such as Coke, fashion, music, entertainment and lifestyle. It is not just the developing economies that are vulnerable to this; France saw a huge outcry when McDonald's first opened its restaurants in Paris.

Business culture

Lean production

Theme 2 looked at production techniques that can lead to greater efficiency, such as TQM and Kaizen and other aspects of lean production. These techniques are sometimes referred to as the 'Japanese way' to indicate their origin. This shows how MNCs have influenced and changed business culture. Initially the Japanese Way hurt many long-established industries which were slow to adapt and failed to survive. Now most manufacturing industries use some or all of these techniques. Globalisation has also changed business culture; as economies become more interconnected, the need for MNCs to become more competitive increases. A more innovative and customer oriented culture has arisen. Technology plays its part as well; improved communications have changed the way businesses operate. The internet and the rise of social media changed the background for businesses. Successful ones have adapted to the new ways and moved forwards.

Tax revenues and transfer pricing

One of the claimed benefits of MNCs is that they will increase a host country's tax revenues. MNCs should in theory pay tax on profits earned in that country. In addition, people employed directly or indirectly will pay taxes on their incomes and on their spending via VAT, excise duties and so on. Government revenues rise, enabling them to increase expenditure and reducing the need for borrowing. This explains why so many countries are keen to attract FDI in the first place.

However, many MNCs do their best to minimise their tax bills, causing much controversy. Starbucks, Google and Amazon have all been attracting negative publicity because of the minimal size of their tax bills, compared to the size of their profit. The companies do this in various ways, including **transfer pricing**.

Tax avoidance

MNCs buy and sell within their organisation. Each national office is a separate profit centre. A company may make a product in Ireland, for sale in continental Europe. To do this, it sells to its sales office in Paris. The Irish office charges a much higher price (transfer price) to its French Office than it might otherwise do, meaning that on paper, the French office shows little or no profit and the Irish office makes a very large profit. This makes sense: the rate of corporation tax (tax on profits) at the time of writing is only 12.5% in Ireland but 33.33% in France. This has the effect of reducing the tax paid by the MNC and increasing its profits at the expense of, in this case, the French Government. To avoid tax in both countries, it can be useful to have another subsidiary in a country (such as Switzerland) which charges no tax on items which just pass through.

> **Transfer pricing** occurs when one part of a MNC in one country transfers (sells) goods or services to another part in another country. The price charged is the 'transfer price'. This may be unrelated to costs incurred and can be set at a level which reduces or cancels out the total tax paid by the MNC.

Each country has a different tax system, with detailed rules of how tax is paid. There are numerous allowances, deductions and exemptions which complicate things further. With the use of some clever tax accountants MNCs can 'minimise', if not avoid, their tax liabilities. The process of avoiding paying tax where tax rates are high is known as tax inversion; it is of great concern to many governments and has led to a numbers of MNCs moving their headquarters to another country.

Apple

In August 2016 Apple was ordered to pay a record-breaking €13bn (£11bn) in back taxes to Ireland. The amount is equal to Ireland's total healthcare bill. The company was presented with the huge bill after the European Commission ruled that a preferential tax deal between Apple and the Irish tax authorities amounted to illegal state aid and was against EU rules.

The commission said the deal allowed Apple to pay a maximum tax rate of just 1%. In 2014, the tech firm paid tax at just 0.005%. The usual rate of corporation tax in Ireland is 12.5%. The commission said Ireland's tax arrangements with Apple between 1991 and 2015 had allowed the US company to attribute sales to a 'head office' that only existed on paper and could not have generated such profits. This meant that Apple avoided tax on almost all the profit generated from its multi-billion euro sales of iPhones and other products, by booking the profits in Ireland rather than the country in which the product was sold.

Apple and Ireland said they intend to appeal against the ruling. Apple's chief executive, Tim Cook, said *"We never asked for, nor did we receive, any special deals. We now find ourselves in the unusual position of being ordered to retroactively pay additional taxes to a government that says we don't owe them any more than we've already paid."* He also warned that future investment by multinationals in Europe could be hit if the ruling is upheld.

Think!

Why do you think the Irish government is on Apple's 'side' in this dispute?

Identify the likely winners and losers if (a) the ruling is upheld and (b) Apple's appeal is successful.

Find out

What has happened to this case since August 2016?

Find and explain another example of a tax dispute involving an MNC.

Exam style question

Location of the world's biggest 500 companies

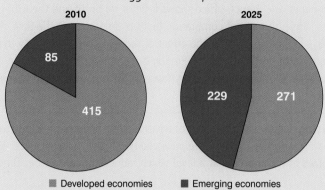

In 2010 there were some 8,000 distinct large companies worldwide with annual revenues of $1bn or more, and three out of four were based in developed economies. It is expected that an additional 7,000 companies will grow to this size by 2025 – and seven out of ten of these new entrants are likely to be based in emerging economies.

By 2025, emerging economies are expected to be home to 229 companies in the Fortune Global 500 (the world's biggest 500 companies), up from 85 in 2010.

1. Explain two possible reasons why an increasing number of new, large companies are forecast to be based in emerging economies. *(8 marks)*

2. Evaluate the possible impact of this on businesses and their customers in (a) developing economies and (b) emerging economies. *(20 marks)*

Chapter 15

Ethics

Terms to revise: stakeholder conflicts (Theme 3), business ethics (Theme 3), environmental protection.

Stakeholder conflicts

Sourcing inputs

Smart phones

The chances are that you own a smart phone; in fact one in every five people on the planet do. The chances are also that you have probably never thought about where they come from. Not about who makes them but what goes into them; what impact does production have on people besides you, the satisfied consumer? A smart phone is a useful device with which to explore the ideas of ethics and stakeholder conflicts.

Each phone contains on average 40 different elements, China is the leading global producer of 22 of the elements used to make smartphones. Each has a story to tell. Here are a few of them…

Copper – There are about 16g of copper in a smartphone, used in the wiring and electronic circuitry. The world's biggest copper ore producer is Chile. The world's fifth largest copper mine, Minera Los Pelambres, is an open-pit mine located 200km north of Santiago and owned by Antofagasta plc. To deal with the waste, the massive El Mauro dam is being built and has been called "the largest toxic chemical dump in Latin America". Apart from the noise and pollution caused by the construction, local communities are deeply concerned over the danger of the dam collapsing in one of the area's many earthquakes. Farmers and fishermen accuse the mining company of altering the watershed, causing rivers to dry up and crops to fail.

Rare earth elements – China produces more than 85% of the world's rare earths, mostly in Inner Mongolia. Processing rare earths is not an environmentally friendly process. The ore often contains radioactive materials and processing generates huge amounts of carcinogenic toxins. One ton of rare earths produces 2000 tons of toxic waste which is pumped into tailings dams. The Baotou Steel tailings pond in the industrial city of Baotou, Inner Mongolia, is the largest on earth and lacks a proper lining. Pollution has already contaminated the local area's water supply and is in danger of reaching the Yellow River, a major drinking water source for much of northern China.

Cobalt – is used in the batteries. Over half of the world's supply comes from The Democratic Republic of Congo. 60% of cobalt is produced by artisanal miners. They are not officially employed by a mining company, but work independently. Artisanal cobalt miners are exposed to heavy metals through dust inhalation and food and water contamination. Despite child labour (some as young as six years old) and dangerous working conditions, artisanal cobalt mining in the DRC is a major driver of economic growth. Some NGOs (non-governmental organisations) argue that businesses should not stop sourcing from the area but rather work to raise standards. Finding other sources will just make the miners even worse off.

Discussion points

Identify as many potential stakeholder conflicts as possible in the production of smart phones.

What might be done to reduce such conflicts?

Does the production of goods and services inevitably produce stakeholder conflicts?

Even a cursory glance at the internet reveals many sites detailing the wrongdoings of MNCs. Some sites specifically monitor individual companies, such as Tescopoly (Tesco), Chevwrong (Chevron), McSpotlight (McDonald's) and March against Monsanto (Monsanto).

> ⚠️ **WATCH OUT!**
>
> Just as you should be wary of what you might find on these companies' own websites, you also need to be careful of sites criticising MNCs. Both are trying to push their own agendas. This is a political minefield; many people see MNCs as villains in the light of anti-globalisation or anti-capitalist stances. The case study above shows the scope for controversy.

Stakeholder conflicts

Critics argue that far from MNCs creating wealth and employment wherever they go, the opposite is true. A range of charges are made against MNCs for acting unethically. All have happened at some time.

- MNCs are driven by an obligation to their owners and shareholders to make a profit. Little if any benefit spills over into the local economy, especially if transfer pricing is used to reduce tax obligations. (See pages 88-9.)

- Local businesses suffer at the hands of the MNCs who cut costs and take away their market share. They mass-produce standardised products, threatening national product variety.

- MNCs may not train local workers to a high level. Expat workers may supply the skills and the locals will provide unskilled labour. R&D facilities may be kept in the home country creating few opportunities for technology or skills transfer.

- Many MNCs enter another country simply to access a new market, so only sales and marketing offices are established. There are few, if any, benefits for local people.

- MNCs are likely to flit from one country to the next, taking whatever incentives are on offer, before moving on to the next and newest low cost location, leaving behind unemployed workers and a weakened economy.

Working conditions

- When they do use local labour, wages and conditions are unsatisfactory, leading to accusations of exploitation and sometimes sweat-shops and child labour.

Environmental degradation

- MNCs cause great damage to the environment by their processes and the transportation of their products. This damage can be short or long term and is usually unsustainable.

- They act as an agent for cultural imperialism which replaces and even destroys the native culture with unwanted products and values.

- They encourage a so-called 'race to the bottom'.

> **Race to the bottom** – a phrase used to describe the way MNCs move to the country that offers the lowest tax rates or the weakest environmental controls. In order to hold onto their MNCs each country will offer them successively more advantageous terms at the expense of their own economy or environment, until the potential benefits of having an MNC are outweighed by the costs.

Pay and working conditions

Local rates of pay

MNCs are often accused of exploiting workers by paying very 'low wages' and keeping employees in sweatshop conditions. This does happen but it can be misleading. Low in comparison to what? We may not be willing to work for wages at that level but that does not mean that those workers are being underpaid or exploited. Wages must be looked at in the context of each economy and each MNC. Many MNCs are using management and production techniques that make them profitable enough to be able to pay well by local standards.

MNC pay

Academic research and international studies do not necessarily support the view that MNCs pay low wages. Jagdish Bhagwati, economist and author of In Defence of Globalisation, backs this point by using empirical studies from Bangladesh, Mexico, Shanghai, Indonesia, Vietnam and elsewhere. The findings are straightforward. Far from exploiting the rock-bottom wage rates generally paid in the poorest countries, multinationals tend to pay above the going rate in the areas in which they are located. In the case of

US multinationals, pay may be 40% to 100% above local wages. The presence of MNCs in the local labour market increases the demand for labour, tending to push up wages generally. Bhagwati said in the Financial Times: *"In my experience, most people in developing countries aspire to work for an MNC."*

Benefits of better pay

There are reasons for this. Higher wages will provide a larger pool of labour from which the employer can choose. This increases the chances of finding workers of the right calibre. Workforce turnover should be reduced, which cuts costs. Well-paid workers may be more motivated and more productive than low-paid ones.

Paul Glewwe, a leading development economist looked at Vietnam and found that the average wage-earner received 23 US cents an hour, but workers in foreign-owned businesses made an average of 42 US cents an hour. When Glewwe conducted his work, 15 per cent of Vietnamese were classified as very poor and 37 per cent as poor. But nobody working for multinationals was classified as very poor and only about 8 per cent were poor. He also found that women seemed to benefit disproportionately from MNCs. *"Two-thirds of workers in foreign-owned businesses in Vietnam are women, and nearly two-thirds are in their 20s, confirming that globalisation is driving social change and female emancipation."*

Suppliers' pay

Of course, this is not to say that all MNCs are wonderful, benevolent organisations dedicated to their worker's welfare. Some MNCs have appalling track records. Despite minimum wage legislation, pay may be well below this level. Attempts to protest or seek legal redress can be met with violence and intimidation. Sometimes it is not the MNCs who are responsible for this but their suppliers. High street names such as Gap, Primark, H&M and Next have all been involved in controversy for using suppliers who pay low wages to their workers. A business such as Gap has thousands of different products; monitoring every stage in the supply chain may be difficult.

Environmental conditions – greenhouse gas emissions

Figure 1: Global greenhouse gas emissions by economic sector

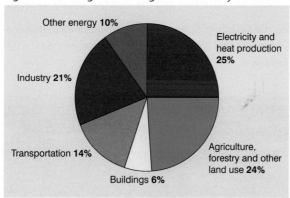

Source: Intergovernmental Panel on Climate Change

Environmental regulation

Greenhouse gas emissions are still high – despite some progress at the 2015 United Nations Climate Change conference in Paris. It is very difficult for governments to agree on the necessary action.

● Governments with low per capita incomes see poverty as a bigger problem than climate change. They want the developed countries to cut back their fossil fuel usage and also to help pay for the investment required to reduce their own carbon emissions. There are still many people in the developed economies who believe that carbon emissions are not responsible for climate change so there is a party political problem. Support for green parties is growing, but fairly slowly.

● Many MNCs find their production costs rising due to environmental regulations in developed countries. One solution is for them to offshore their biggest carbon emitting processes to countries with less regulation (most of which are emerging and developing economies). This helps to keep them competitive, but simply shifts their polluting activities to less-regulated locations.

Table 1: Carbon emissions per country, 2014

Country	Million metric tonnes
China	10,541
USA	5,335
India	2,342
Russia	1,766
Germany	767
UK	415
Source: UN	

Table 2: Carbon emissions per capita, 2014

Country	Metric tonnes
China	7.6
USA	16.7
India	1.8
Russia	12.4
Germany	9.5
UK	6.4
Source: UN	

Who emits most?

Show your understanding

1. Explain why it is difficult to reduce carbon emissions quickly.

2. Some of the energy used to manufacture Apple products in China will come from coal fired power stations. If China decided to ban the use of coal, how would Apple react and how would customers be affected?

3. How might governments adopt a fair way to address the problem?

Emissions from farms

It is very difficult to assess the true cost of environmental damage caused by business activity. Figures for annual damage by industry vary from $2 trillion to $4.7 trillion. A 2015 report by Trucost, for the UN, placed the cost of industrialised farming at $3 trillion. The research found that livestock farming costs the environment $1.81 trillion per year. Beef production in Brazil accounted for the most costly environmental impacts at $596m, mainly due to deforestation to clear land for pasture. Pork production in China cost $327m, mostly due to direct land-use conversion and the supply chain for feed production.

One of the more unfortunate and catastrophic examples of environmental damage was the BP oil spill in the Gulf of Mexico. For many people this is symptomatic of the careless way in which big business has a negative impact on the environment.

One of the more unfortunate and catastrophic examples of environmental damage was the BP oil spill in the Gulf of Mexico.

Waste disposal

Toxic waste

Mining

Grasberg mine is owned by Freeport, the world's lowest-cost copper producer. It is the largest gold mine and the third largest copper mine in the world, located in the heart of Mount Jaya in West Papua. It is home to three of the world's eight remaining equatorial glaciers. It is a sacred site for the indigenous people inhabiting the region and depending on its ecosystem to survive. The mining process has destroyed huge sections of the mountain top leaving a massive open pit visible from space. The mine uses more than a billion gallons of water a month and has been accused of dumping 230,000 tonnes of toxic waste into the Ajkwa Rivers each day, killing all plant life along its banks and contaminating drinking water supplies. Both Freeport and its partner Rio Tinto have been excluded from the investment portfolio of The Government Pension Fund of Norway, the world's second-largest pension fund, due to criticism over the environmental damage caused by the Grasberg mine.

1. Why would the Indonesian government allow Freeport and Rio Tinto to dump toxic waste in this way? Explain possible reasons.
2. What would happen if shareholders agreed with the Norwegian government?

Waste disposal is expensive. In the UK, it is one of the fastest growing sectors of the economy. Also, regulating waste disposal is expensive for governments that get little tax revenue. Without tight regulation, it is very tempting for businesses to choose the cheapest solution. This may be short sighted, perhaps leading to loss of reputation or added expense in the future. They may face compensation demands.

Supply chain considerations – working conditions

Complex supply chains

Charges levelled at MNCs refer to the exploitation of labour including sweatshops, use of child labour, anti-trade union practices, poor health and safety. Many household names such as Nike, Gap and Primark have been accused of one or more of these. It is perhaps important at this stage to distinguish between MNCs that set up their own production plants and those that buy from local suppliers. It is much easier to control working conditions with the former than with the latter. Complex supply chains can sometimes hide very real problems. It is fair to say that some MNCs are not always as strict or as careful about their source of supplies as they could be.

Child labour

MNC seed companies such as Monsanto, Syngenta and Bayer have been accused of exploiting child labour on Indian cotton farms, where they work long hours and are exposed to harmful pesticides. According to UNICEF, an estimated 250 million children aged between 11 and 14 and 60 million between 5 and 11 work for a living. While most MNCs have nothing to do with the direct exploitation of child labour, many suppliers are known to be involved.

Example

In Malawi, one of the poorest nations, an estimated 75% of the population are directly or indirectly employed by the tobacco industry, which accounts for two thirds of its foreign exchange earnings. Malawi has an estimated 1.4 million child labourers, one of the highest incidences of child labour in Africa. Many of them work on tobacco farms for their families who are tenants and produce the crop for their landlord who sells it on to the big tobacco companies. Many of the children suffer from high levels of nicotine poisoning. The unregulated use of pesticides has led to further accusations of malpractice on many tobacco estates. The International Tobacco Growers Association opposes the use of child labour. Nevertheless, some of the world's biggest MNCs buy their tobacco from these sources. They use their monopsony power to drive down prices, depressing wages and perpetuating the need for children to help the family out by working rather than going to school. BAT claim that they are acting responsibly and have co founded the Eliminating Child Labour in Tobacco Growing Foundation (ECLT). ECLT's initial projects were budgeted at US$2.3 million over four years and include projects such as building schools, planting trees, and constructing shallow wells. Critics say that this is just a PR exercise and that in the same period, the tobacco companies received nearly US$40 million by benefiting from child labour.

Health and safety

MNCs are sometimes charged with failing to ensure that proper health and safety standards are applied. In developing and emerging economies laws and regulations may not be as stringent, or as rigorously applied, as they are in developed economies. This may encourage some MNCs to cut corners and save money. In some cases the consequences for the workforce and host country can be very serious indeed. Perhaps the most infamous example is that of Bhopal and the Union Carbide plant where a lethal mixture of gas and toxins leaked out in 1984. The cause was poor safety standards. An estimated 20,000 have died since the accident and another 100,000 to 200,000 people are estimated to have permanent injuries due to the gas leak.

The mining industry in particular attracts much controversy over some of its working practices. In Mexico, widows of Mexican miners killed by an explosion in a coal mine in 2006 sued owner Grupo Mexico. They are alleging that the deaths were caused by unsafe working practices which caused the explosion to happen. In 2016, the Mexican government had still not fully investigated the disaster.

Human rights

Elsewhere Walmart, despite some recent environmental changes for the better, is still accused by some as remaining anti-union and offering low pay and limited benefits. It strongly opposes living wage initiatives.

> **Find out**
> Some MNCs are adopting ethical standards for their workforce and making a genuine effort to improve working conditions. Find an example of significant improvement and explain the business strategy behind it.

Marketing considerations – product labelling and promotional activities

Legal, honest, decent and truthful

The Advertising Standards Authority (ASA) is the UK's independent regulator of advertising across all media. It is famous for its slogan 'Legal, honest, decent and truthful'. In some countries, including the UK, marketing must comply with certain standards. If adverts do not, the ASA has the power to ban them. Labelling must be accurate: there are many examples of labels that purport to tell the truth but are actually misleading in subtle ways. This is common in both food and skin care labelling.

> **Example**
> In May 2016, a TV ad for Captain Morgan rum featured a party on an old-fashioned wooden sailing ship. A man with Captain Morgan's face, from the advertiser's logo, superimposed over his own was shown partying and generally having a good time. A complaint that this was irresponsible because it associated alcohol with having a good time and increasing self-confidence was upheld by the ASA. The advert was never shown again.

Codes of practice

Not all countries have such a strong code and even if they do, there are grey and controversial areas. For example, should children's TV carry adverts for sweets or toys? Should supermarkets promote fattening foods with special offers? Should adverts for cars mention top speeds that are far in excess of the speed limit? What do you think?

These examples may seem mild; some may not see a problem, but some promotional activities are questionable and some clearly inappropriate. Consider this: nearly 80% of the world's one billion smokers now live in low- and middle-income countries, a figure that continues to increase. In the 20th century, some 100 million people were killed by tobacco use. If current trends continue, tobacco is predicted to kill a billion people in the 21st century.

In Indonesia alone there are 21 million child smokers. There is little to stop companies promoting cigarettes to young people. In countries such as Nigeria, Ukraine and Brazil, tobacco companies have sponsored club nights or parties aimed at attracting new young users. In Russia, attempts to entice women smokers have included packaging made to look like jewel-encrusted perfume bottles and even selling cigarettes branded by the fashion house Yves Saint Laurent. In some African countries attractive young ladies stand outside football grounds, handing out free cigarettes to young boys and girls.

Ethical issues

Many MNCs have done much to improve their actions whether pushed by public opinion, legislation or just plain altruism. For example Nike is now regarded as a good example of how to be transparent and ensure good corporate responsibility.

A report by Robert Stern and others at the University of Michigan concluded: *"However, as an empirical matter, …there is virtually no careful and systematic evidence demonstrating that, as a generality, multinational firms adversely affect their workers, provide incentives to worsen working conditions, pay lower wages than in alternative employment, or repress worker rights. In fact, there is a very large body of empirical evidence indicating that the opposite is the case."*

Other studies support this conclusion; the idea that MNCs all exploit labour and treat their workers badly does not bear scrutiny. This does not mean that such practices do not happen. They do; the supply chain for many large MNCs is very complex and it is not always possible to monitor every small supplier effectively. Besides the case studies in this chapter on events in Malawi and Indonesia, there are many other examples of exploitative actions by MNCs. It is a mistake to look at MNCs as all being the same.

MNCs and Orang Utans

Oil companies have been accused of causing destruction to rainforests and wildlife by secretly adding palm oil to diesel that is sold to millions of UK motorists. Only 15 per cent of the palm oil comes from sustainable resources. The rest comes from land previously occupied by rainforest.

Large areas of rainforest are destroyed each year, by companies seeking to take advantage of the world's growing demand for biofuels. They produce fewer emissions than fossil fuels because crops absorb carbon dioxide as they grow. It is not just the oil companies at fault here; many food products that you buy at your local supermarket also use palm oil as an ingredient.

The problem is that clearing rainforest to create biofuel plantations releases vast quantities of carbon stored in trees and soil. It takes up to 840 years for a palm oil plantation to soak up the carbon emitted when rainforest is burnt to plant the crop. Some three-quarters of these new plantations are alleged to have been planted illegally.

Indonesia has the greatest rate of deforestation, losing an area the size of Wales every year. The orang-utan, which lives in the rain forest, has been pushed to the brink of extinction in some areas. Indonesia is now the third-largest CO_2 emitter, after China and the US.

1. Explain why palm oil is valuable on world markets. *(4 marks)*

2. Identify the ethical issues associated with buying palm oil from Indonesia. *(8 marks)*

3. Use Porter's five forces to assess the extent to which MNC strategies are driven
   (a) by competitive forces and (b) by shareholder pressure. *(12 marks)*

4. Evaluate possible ethical solutions to palm oil problems. *(20 marks)*

Chapter 16
Controlling MNCs

Viiankiaapa

In 2011, the British-listed mining company, Anglo American, discovered huge deposits of nickel at Viiankiaapa in Finland. This is in a wetlands area of 65 sq km providing a habitat for 21 endangered bird species in the Arctic Circle. The Finnish government gave permission for mining to proceed because of the need for jobs in Lapland. However, Anglo-American did not observe the government's requests to monitor wildlife carefully and to cause minimal damage. Mining is now causing serious damage to the wetlands. Hannah Aho, a conservation expert for the Finnish Association for Nature Conservation, said *"Viiankiaapa is not only a unique area in Finland, but in Europe."* In 2015 the European Parliament asked the Commission in Brussels to investigate. In August 2016 all drilling was paused pending a Supreme Court Ruling. Anglo American cannot go ahead without clear legal permission.

Discussion points

What could have been done to limit the damage?

How might local people have reacted to what happened?

Costs vs. benefits

This chapter looks at whether it is possible to control MNCs and prevent developments that are unpopular. This is not always possible; some MNCs as we have seen are vast, powerful and rich organisations. They also bring many benefits to their host nations. Developing economies in particular find it hard to stand up to MNCs and in many cases accept the harm they cause because the benefits are much greater.

By their very nature MNCs are hard to control because they transcend national boundaries. There is no such thing as a 'world government' or 'world court' that can prevent MNCs from doing what they want or force them to modify their behaviour. As we shall see, some efforts have been made by the UN and other bodies to exert some influence over MNCs but with varied success. There is a trade-off between conservation and the need for scarce resources. Such control as there is comes from a range of factors.

Source of control	Ways of achieving a degree of control
Political influence	Governments may be influenced by powerful MNCs but they may also be concerned about public opinion or about the need for economic projects that generate income. They can through the planning laws prevent certain types of development, within their own borders.
Legal control	Governments can use their power to enforce the law or regulations that may prevent MNCs from the most unpopular activities, within their own borders.
Pressure groups	Can mobilise public opinion and publicise their concerns through the media. By lobbying government bodies they may have some influence but they cannot control what happens.
Social media	Makes communication easy for pressure groups and individuals and may influence public opinion; can be used to damage MNCs reputations so that they respond to the weight of public opinion in order to avoid falling sales.

In practice it is often a combination of these factors that comes in to operation. Public opinion can lead to the creation of pressure groups which may mount media campaigns to persuade the MNC to modify its actions or persuade governments to intervene or bring about legal proceedings. Given the right circumstances even the biggest MNC can be controlled.

Show your understanding

Explain the options open to the Finnish government when Anglo-American first proposed mining.

Political influence

Power

Much will depend on the relative power of the MNC and host country. Probably the strongest country in relation to MNCs, and so most able to regulate their actions, is China. Its huge market with a potential 1.3 billion customers acts as a powerful incentive for businesses to accept the limitations and controls of the strongly regulated Chinese state. Even though the restrictions on foreign businesses in China were relaxed slightly after they joined the WTO, all forms of business require state approval before starting. Whether it is a joint venture, a representative office or a wholly owned foreign enterprise, the relevant paperwork, license and approval must be gained. These of course, can be revoked by the state at any time.

Google

Google China was founded in 2005. Soon after, Google agreed to accept Chinese censorship of its search engine, and to self-censor itself on certain issues. Many people outside China voiced their disapproval. The Chinese government was particularly annoyed that Google searches could access information on China's policies in Tibet and on the views of Tibetans.

The Chinese government was never very happy with Google, and encouraged Chinese people to use the home-grown search engine, Baidu. After a hacking attack from within China, Google decided not to accept any more censoring of searches and said it would pull out of China altogether if necessary. It began to redirect Chinese searches to Google Hong Kong where laws are different.

All governments can control business activity to a certain extent and there are many ways of doing this. It may take the form of a licensing agreement as in the case of India and China or the government can insist on a joint venture before allowing access to the market. Restrictions can be placed on the degree of foreign ownership. MNCs can be required to use a certain percentage of labour; controls can be placed on the number of foreign personnel allowed into the country and so on. In reality much depends on the relative power of the state and the MNC. The Chinese government certainly wants MNCs to have a presence there but it also wants to develop its own MNCs, so restrictions on foreign firms are increasing.

Countries that are hungry for FDI may be less fussy than China. India in particular is very keen to attract FDI but there are many others that may offer easier entry. Developed economies expect MNCs to abide by their own regulations and may challenge significant regulatory breaches.

Compensation

● The USA forced BP to pay $20.8bn as settlement over the Deepwater Horizon oil spill in 2010. They also had to spend $32bn to clean up the Gulf area following the disaster. However, it subsequently transpired that much of this sum was tax deductible, costing US taxpayers $10 billion.

Taxation

● In Australia the government has attempted to gain more of the lucrative revenues from the mining industry by levying a supertax on MNC profits. This was passed in 2012 but faced legal challenges by the mining companies. It was repealed in 2014 following a change of government.

Corruption

Corruption is a fact of life in many countries. MNCs seek political influence and may collaborate with politicians for mutual benefit, particularly in less developed economies. Effectively they are buying the opportunity to do business. Corruption has a detrimental influence on the whole economy, the people and the environment. The Democratic Republic of Congo (DRC) was ranked 147 out of 168 nations on Transparency International's 2015 Corruption Perception Index. It is rich in minerals and as with other countries, mining companies bid for licences to be allowed to mine. The payment should go to the state

Corruption is a fact of life in many countries and has a detrimental influence on the whole economy, the people and the environment.

but it finds its way to those individuals and politicians who control the state. The annual loss to the budget from these practices is estimated to be about $1.73bn. The GDP of the DRC in 2015 was $35.24bn. With stronger and more established political systems, corruption is usually less of a problem and MNCs have to follow the established procedures. Top of the index was Denmark with the UK in 10th place.

Transparency International

> **Find out**
> Transparency International keeps track of progress with corruption. Find out where it is a serious problem and where it should now be coming under control. The index covers the past four years.

China is 83rd, despite a recent government clampdown by President Xi and the Communist Party on corruption. The giving of lavish gifts was all part of doing business in China but this has almost halted after a two year campaign, much to the dismay of many luxury western retailers. One leading Swiss watch company said that before the anti-corruption campaign as many as 65 out of every 100 of their watches were sold in China. Today, only 25 in 100 go to Chinese customers.

Corruption tends to weaken the power of governments. Vested interests control them and reduce their ability to act independently. But in some cases, MNCs will be drawn to corrupt economies because they can get what they want by paying for it.

Footloose MNCs

MNCs that have the potential to shift their activities to other countries further reduce government power because their departure could reduce economic growth. The host economy will have various economic problems, such as a rise in unemployment, lower future tax revenues and reduced export earnings. In short the loss of an MNC means a reversal of many of the benefits associated with the arrival of an MNC in the first place.

Legal control

Going to court

All countries have a legal framework under which businesses must operate. The effectiveness of legal frameworks varies considerably; much depends on the individual country and its governance. One way of controlling the behaviour of an MNC is to seek legal redress by taking the company to court. This worked for the USA with BP's Deepwater Horizon explosion but fails sometimes because MNCs are not under the control of any one legal system. It can be difficult to hold a parent company liable for the actions of one of its subsidiary companies.

Example

In October 2008, a lawsuit against Chevron Nigeria Ltd., a subsidiary of Chevron USA Inc., went to trial in a Californian court. It was alleged that the subsidiary company had been responsible for human rights violations and that the parent company was liable. The court decided that this was not the case and exonerated Chevron. The company is facing an ongoing legal battle over its alleged pollution of the Ecuadorian rainforest, displacement of indigenous peoples and a legacy of cancers and birth defects caused by the contamination. The proceedings have been going on since 1993; at the time of writing it has still not been fully settled.

Advertising standards in India

In some countries the legal system can be difficult to use and success is uncertain. When attempting to tackle large and wealthy MNCs, the legal proceedings can be lengthy and very costly. Sometimes though, legal proceedings are effective. The Advertising Standards Council of India (ASCI) successfully upheld complaints about PepsiCo, Britannia, Pizza Hut, Amazon, LG Electronics, Voltas, Axis Bank, AirAsia and Flipkart, among others, for running misleading advertising campaigns. In 2014, 12 Japanese suppliers of car parts were fined by the Chinese courts, for price fixing.

Show your understanding

The Volkswagen (VW) emissions scandal is now a major legal dispute in several countries. VW reached a $15.3bn settlement in 2016 with lawyers representing US owners of its cars that were caught up in the scandal, plus certain regulators. The US Department of Justice has launched a criminal investigation into VW's actions, and prosecutors in Germany are looking at, among other things, the conduct of Martin Winterkorn, the former chief executive. Spain has launched a case alleging fraud and criminal damage to the environment. If found guilty, VW could face heavy fines. Under Spanish law, its local subsidiary may be forced to close. In total the company has set aside €16.2bn to cover scandal-related costs.

Court action

VW allowed a procedure that contravened regulations on emissions. What effect would this have on (a) customers, (b) the general public, (c) its reputation and (d) its sales?

Anti-competitive practices

Regulatory authorities such as the Competition and Markets Authority (CMA) in the UK, and the EU equivalent in Brussels, can sometimes control anti-competitive practices that raise prices. They have far reaching powers and the ability to levy fines of up to 10% of a firm's turnover if they act against the public interest. The EU Commission is currently investigating both Google and Microsoft. Both the CMA and the EU can block mergers that would increase the size of an MNC if they deem it against the public interest. The EU recently blocked a proposed £10bn takeover of O2 by CK Hutchison, the company which operates Three.

Regulatory control

Examples

- 2016: GSK has been under investigation since 2011 in a so-called pay-for-delay case, where it is alleged to have paid several smaller pharmaceutical companies to delay selling their cheaper version of the antidepressant Paxil, also known as Seroxat.

- 2015: Telecoms firm Orange was fined €350m (£254m) for abusing its market dominance in France.

- 2015: Pfizer and a UK company called Flynn Pharma were found to have charged "excessive and unfair prices" for an anti-epilepsy drug, inflating the NHS drugs bill by tens of millions of pounds.

- 2014: The EU competition authorities ordered RyanAir to pay back €10m in illegal state aid on the grounds that state aid gave them an unfair advantage and distorted competition on several routes.

Even countries in such dire straits as Zimbabwe are sometimes able to use the regulatory authorities to good effect. The Zimbabwean subsidiary of BAT (British American Tobacco) had to change its policies after they were found to have been using predatory pricing against new entrants into the market.

Legal costs

Powerful MNCs have the resources and deep pockets to fight long and costly legal battles, making it difficult to apply legal or regulatory controls. Even if a decision is secured to control the MNC, it can be delayed for a long time. The EU's battle with Microsoft and the Chevron dispute mentioned earlier have been going on for over two decades. Weak governments in poor countries have little chance to enforce regulations.

Pressure groups

Public opinion, pressure groups and the media can work together to highlight problems. Public opinion leads to the creation of pressure groups which can in turn influence public opinion. Pressure groups can use the media to publicise their actions, which may further influence public opinion.

Public opinion

Over recent years, public opinion has influenced the behaviour of many MNCs. This is particularly true for those companies that rely on consumer loyalty and their brand name. Think of Nike: after much damaging publicity over sweatshops and the use of child labour in some of its suppliers' factories in the 90s, sales dropped as the public showed their disapproval. Similar allegations were made about Gap and both businesses did change their supply chain policies to placate customers. More recently Primark has faced similar problems following reports made on TV and in the media, although these had less impact; evidently low prices make up for some ethical doubts.

> **Pressure groups** attempt to influence MNC policy and especially governmental legislation, regarding their particular concerns and priorities.

One area in which pressure groups are particularly active is the environment. Some large companies have failed to practise good environmental management and been targeted by campaigners. Pressure groups often represent many consumers and widespread opinion; it can be important for a company to maintain good relations with them. Greenpeace is perhaps the best-known environmental pressure group in the UK.

Greenpeace, Palm Oil & Unilever

Greenpeace ran a campaign to highlight the environmental impact of the global increase in demand for palm oil. They have campaigned against companies such as Unilever, which produces many of Britain's best-known household brands such as Flora and Stork margarines, Dove toiletries and Persil. At that time, Unilever was the world's biggest user of palm oil.

In 2008, Unilever announced that the palm oil they use would be certified sustainable by 2015. It also said that Unilever was supporting the call for an immediate moratorium on any further deforestation in Indonesia for palm oil plantations. In 2009 Unilever terminated a $32.6 million contract with one of their suppliers, the Indonesian group Sinar Mas, after  proof that they were involved in the destruction of rainforest. In 2010 Unilever said it would not be buying supplies from the Indonesian company Duta Palma, following a BBC documentary showing Duta Palma staff clearing rainforests for palm oil estates.

The Indonesian Minister for Agriculture has called for environmental groups to "stop demonising palm oil."

Campaigning

Greenpeace continues to campaign on this issue and in 2016 published a report, 'Cutting Deforestation out of the Palm Oil Supply Chain'. This is a scorecard focusing on 14 global consumer brands with No Deforestation commitments. It is particularly critical of Johnson & Johnson, PepsiCo and Colgate-Palmolive.

1. Explain why Unilever might have decided to use only sustainable palm oil.

2. Explore possible reasons for the Indonesian Minister's comments on Greenpeace's campaign.

Social media

The internet is becoming more and more important in monitoring and controlling MNCs. In the previous chapter we mentioned sites, such as Tescopoly and Chevwrong, that critically report the activities of particular companies. These are very useful ways of disseminating information and rallying support and undoubtedly have some influence. More recently Twitter, YouTube and Facebook have been used to publicise issues. It is now possible to motivate individuals in a way that was impossible before the creation of the internet and social media. As a result, more MNCs have tried to avoid ethical scandals.

Disseminating information

At the end of March 2010, Nestlé followed Unilever and bowed to pressure to make the palm oil used in the manufacture of products such as KitKat, Aero and Quality Street more eco-friendly. This followed a guerrilla campaign waged against it on the internet. The centrepiece of this campaign was a spoof advert against KitKat, mimicking its 'Have a Break' advert. It showed an office worker biting into a KitKat containing an orangutan finger, which dripped blood onto a computer keyboard. This was a reference to the damage done by the unsustainable use of palm oil to orangutans, which live only on the heavily deforested islands of Borneo and Sumatra.

Over 1 million people watched the advert on YouTube and many of them posted angry messages on Nestlé's Facebook page – substituting the word Killer for KitKat. Greenpeace also disrupted Nestlé's annual general meeting. Protesting 'orangutans' greeted shareholders and, inside the building, activists unfurled banners with the message: "Nestlé, give the orangutans a break".

Positive promotion

Social media works both ways. MNCs have long been good at handling the media and putting their point of view across. The same applies to social media where positive promotional campaigns are just as likely to reach consumers as activist campaigns from pressure groups.

Examples

In Australia a school student Angelina Popovski started an online petition to stop the sale of eggs from caged hens. It was so successful that some retailers such as Aldi banned them from their stores

Petitions

More than a million campaigners signed a petition calling for Benetton, an Italian clothing company, to contribute towards a compensation fund for victims of the Rana Plaza factory collapse in Bangladesh that killed around 1100 people. Benetton later contributed $1.1m.

Mumsnet, a UK website aimed at parents, particularly women, runs a series of campaigns such as the 'Lads' mags: out of children's sight'. This persuaded major retailers such as Sainsbury's, Waitrose, Asda, Morrison's, BP, Tesco and the Co-op Group to keep magazines with overtly sexualised cover images above children's eyelines in shops.

Self regulation

A growing number of companies are taking steps to control and modify their own behaviour by adopting and strengthening their own CSR policies. Some join an umbrella organisation such as the UK government backed ETI (Ethical Trading Initiative) and EITI (Extractive Industries Transparency Initiative), or the Fairtrade Foundation and adopt their ethical codes.

CSR by itself is of little importance in regulating the behaviour of an MNC. A quick glance at the websites of the bottom five companies in the Covalence 2009 Ethical Rankings table will show that they all have a comprehensive CSR policy in place! Yet clearly some MNCs, whether for reasons of commercial pressure or altruism, are responding to public opinion and attempting to change the way they operate. Marks and Spencer is a case in point.

Find out

In 2007, M&S set out a programme to:

● become carbon neutral

● send no waste to landfill

● extend sustainable sourcing

● help improve the lives of people in the supply chain

● help customers and employees to live a healthier life-style.

By 2013, they reckoned they had met their targets. A new Plan A 2020 is in place with very detailed objectives for all aspects of the business. The plan looks hard to fudge.

Look at the M&S website and select Plan A 2020. Evaluate the likely significance of three of their objectives.

Ethical codes

The Ethical Trading Initiative (ETI) is an alliance of companies, trade unions and voluntary organisations. All members of ETI agree to adopt the ETI code of labour practice which is based on the standards of the UN's International Labour Organisation (ILO). Their aim is to improve the lives of workers across the globe, all those who make or grow consumer goods – everything from tea to T-shirts, from flowers to footballs. The purpose of EITI is to make companies and governments publicly disclose how much they earn and the amount they pay to the developing countries where they operate.

Brand image

The Fairtrade Foundation is the independent non-profit organisation that licenses the use of the Fair Trade Mark on products in the UK that comply with internationally agreed Fairtrade standards. The businesses that join initiatives like these must adhere to the standards set down by the organisation. The tradeoff is likely to be an enhanced brand image in the eyes of consumers and potentially increased sales.

One drawback of ethical codes is that they may focus the MNC's attention on addressing just one issue while ignoring other problem areas. Their efforts require careful scrutiny.

Conclusion: can MNCs be controlled?

The extent to which it is possible to control MNCs depends upon the circumstances and the relative power each agent holds. For example the US government is much more likely to be able to control or modify MNC behaviour than the Nigerian government. Similarly, the legal and regulatory framework in the EU is much tougher and more comprehensive than in many developing nations. Some companies such as Shell can withstand pressure to change. Small MNCs may never be noticed by public opinion or pressure groups. Some actually have a genuine desire to behave responsibly and take great care to do so.

Many businesses are driven purely by the profit motive and prioritise shareholder value. Institutional investors (pension funds and insurance companies) may show little interest in ethical issues, particularly those that relate to overseas subsidiaries. Bonuses based on share price performance may matter more to senior managers than pressure for decent wage rates and working conditions. Shareholders mainly want to see profits being made and a return on their investment. However, some shareholders do take an active

Share Action

interest in how the company is run and do try to influence the direction of MNCs. Share Action is a pressure group which helps to empower shareholders by providing them with the tools and information to take on the directors, improve corporate behaviour and protect the environment.

Reputation

Where reputation is important, a scandal is likely to do lasting damage. Companies like Disney or Mothercare depend on their reputation with the buying public. On the other hand major mining companies and commodity traders such as Glencore do not deal with the public. Their customers are other MNCs that are primarily concerned with commodity prices.

MNCs are now much more likely to amend their behaviour than previously. A combination of globalisation, modern communications and technology and social media means that their activities are now much easier to observe and scrutinise. Public opinion is more swiftly engaged and mobilised and many businesses are now more sensitive to that pressure. More and more MNCs are claiming to act responsibly, either as a selling point, or from genuine altruism. Governments are able to use both legislation and direct control to modify the actions of some MNCs.

Inappropriate waste disposal

However, not all governments are willing to control aspects of MNC behaviour; some are simply corrupt or inefficient or lack the will to try. For some governments there can be a trade-off between appeasing public opinion and the need for the economic stimulus that MNCs can bring. Inevitably, some MNCs continue to behave in a way that is less than desirable. Pollution and inappropriate waste disposal still happen and pressure groups are still active.

There is no clear cut answer to the question "Can multinationals be controlled?" However, there is some evidence that some MNCs may face increasing competition.

Kenya

Recent developments suggest that some MNCs may need to adapt more. In 2008 Nestlé began work on an investment programme across 21 countries in equatorial Africa. The company was planning for expected growth of the middle class. In the oil exporting countries – Nigeria, Sudan and Angola – a significant middle class is emerging. Nigeria is thought to have 8 million middle class households already, forecast to reach 21 million by 2030. Nestlé's efforts there have been worthwhile. However, in Kenya, a very different situation has emerged. Two thirds of Nairobi's residents live in informal settlements. (This is a polite description of shanty towns, some of which are slums.) Nestlé is not doing well there because local companies are fighting back. They have local appeal and have put time and money into raising product standards and creating their own brands, tailored to suit local people. Regional supermarket chains are creating their own cheap and reliable brands. They are competing successfully with Nestlé. UK brand Weetabix, now owned by China, thinks it has 80% of the Kenyan cereal market.

What advantages might new entrants have? How might they succeed in competing with big MNCs?

MNC products

Modern life is built around products of MNCs such as Apple, Shell, Sony, Ford, MacDonald's, Bosch, Yamaha, H&M and so on. Without them, choice would be limited and innovation would be well below the level we take for granted. Very few people would like to see the back of MNCs. But there are numerous examples of MNCs that acted appallingly, both in the past and in the present. The enormous size and economic strength of some MNCs compared to the national income of their host countries does little to dispel fears about their impact.

Exam style question

Margaret Hodge, Public Accounts Committee chairman, said of Google in 2013 "You are a company that says you do no evil, and I think that you do do evil in that you use smoke and mirrors to avoid paying tax," adding that the company engaged in "devious, calculated and, in my view, unethical behaviour."

Evaluate the extent to which the actions of MNCs can be controlled. *(20 marks)*

Current trends

Most of this book has been about the astonishing growth of trade and globalisation over the past 40 years. But there are signs that the global economy is now changing and there is great uncertainty about what future trends may look like. On page 40, Figure 2 shows trade as a percentage of global GDP

Both the IMF and the World Bank have cited several reasons.

● Slow economic growth in the Eurozone and in Japan is leading to deflation which can act like a trap, making it harder for policymakers to stimulate consumer spending and investment.

● Many developed countries have prioritised paying off government debt (arising from the 2008-9 financial crisis), rather than stimulating their economies by increasing government spending.

● Shifting political opinions may lead to more protectionism. This could shrink export markets and discourage the growth of international trade.

● New technologies such as robots and 3-D printing could make re-shoring attractive to businesses.

Example

Tucked away in Gloucestershire is Renishaw, a company that makes 3D printing machines and industrial measurement devices. These are potential game-changers that make additive manufacturing possible. Their work will in time transform the efficient manufacture of components. Renishaw spends 12% of sales revenue on R&D; of that 65% is spent on new product development. Their biggest customers are Asian electronics businesses.

Explain how this could make re-shoring easier.

There are policies that could be used to encourage trade:

● Less emphasis on austerity policies; spending on infrastructure, training and public services to encourage economic growth and competitiveness

● Raising minimum wages, to increase consumer spending power

● Continuing trade negotiations to reduce trade barriers

● Opposing protectionism both nationally and globally.

Figure 1: World trade volume and world GDP growth, % change, 1981-2016

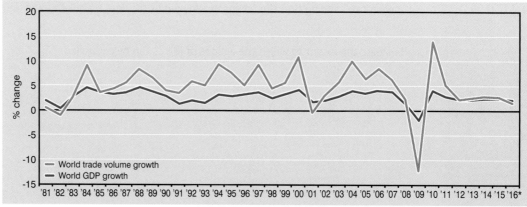

Source: WTO Secretariat for trade, consensus estimates for GDP   *Estimate

Answers / Interpreting index numbers

Answers to numerical questions

Page 27, Q2, US$2,500.

Page 58, Q1, A tourist from the UK would have to pay £7 more. A tourist from the Eurozone would have to pay €17 more.

Page 60, Q1,£41,666; Q2, £1,812 more.

These questions are not very difficult to calculate, are they? But take care to use each number you are given in the right way – that is more tricky.

Index numbers

The specifications for this course require you to be able to interpret index numbers. On page 16, Table 1 uses index numbers to show how the costs of air transport and phone calls have fallen since 1930. This is the kind of data where index numbers are most useful. They allow us to compare changes in two quite different variables.

The key factor is the base year – always 100. What the index number tells you is that the price of air travel in 2004 is just 12% of what it was in 1930. Index numbers measure percentage changes from the base year, so that changes in air travel prices can be compared with changes in phone call prices.

In this table, the prices of both air transport and phone calls will have been affected by inflation. The technologies involved are different. But comparison is still possible if both prices are shown as index numbers.

An index number is not the same as an index. Table 3 on page 42 shows the Ease of doing business Index. This has nothing to do with index numbers. It is much more like the index at the end of this book. It ranks countries so that they can be compared, but the rankings have no base value.

Index